MW01118570

TOTAL QUALITY TOOLS
FOR HEALTH CARE™

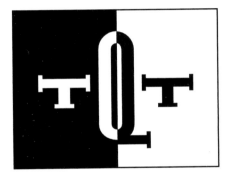

TOTAL QUALITY TRANSFORMATION®

Edited by:
Sandra K. Murray
and
O. Byron Murray

PRODUCTION NOTES

TQT® is a family of products based on our current understanding of the theory, process, and tools of continuous improvement. The *TQT* product line will grow, expand, and improve as we continue to learn.

Products currently available are:
Foundations for Leaders*
Improvement Guide*
Improvement Tools*
Alignment Guide*
Team Skills
Strategic Quality Planning Guide
Pocket Tools*
Total Quality Tools for Education
Total Quality Tools for Service & Manufacturing

* K-12 Educational version available.

Total Quality Tools for Health Care © PQ Systems, Inc., first printing, version 1 November, 1997.
ISBN 1-882683-04-8
Production notes: Printing by Prime Printing, Dayton, OH
Design generated on Power Macintosh 7600 using Adobe *PageMaker*™ and Macromedia *FreeHand*™ and Prescience *Expressionist*™

Total Quality Transformation materials are copyrighted by PQ Systems, Inc.
Total Quality Transformation and *TQT* are registered trademarks of PQ Systems, Inc.

01/02   100
© PQ Systems, Inc.
Health Care

TABLE OF CONTENTS

Acknowledgments

PQ Systems, Inc., wishes to acknowledge the contributions of the following to the development of the *Total Quality Transformation®* materials:

The design team:
Melinda J. Ball, PQ Systems, Inc.
Michael J. Cleary, Ph.D, PQ Systems, Inc., and Wright State University
Susan Leddick, Ed.D., Profound Knowledge Resources, Inc.
Carole J. Schwinn, Jackson Community College
David R. Schwinn, Transformation Project
Elaine Torres, Partners in Profound Knowledge, Inc.

Special thanks to Dennis Cleary and Linda O'Malley for their role in the production of the materials.

Other contributions were made by the following PQ Systems employees:
Barbara A. Cleary, Ph.D., Gordon Constable, Ph.D., Sally Duncan, Jacqueline Graham, Ph.D., and Dan Inman

ABOUT PQ SYSTEMS

Productivity-Quality Systems, Inc. is a full-service firm dedicated to helping customers continuously improve their organizations. We offer a comprehensive network of products and services designed to improve quality, productivity, and competitive position for all industries. The full line of improvement products and services from PQ Systems includes:

SQCpack® **for Windows**™ combines powerful SPC techniques with flexibility and ease of use. In addition to variables, attributes, and Pareto charting capabilities, *SQCpack* for Windows features multiple identifiers, corrective actions, multiple characteristics, SQC Quality Advisor,™ extensive cause and note fields, filtering, and ODBC. You can even enter preventive, instructional, or corrective action procedures to help you comply with ISO 9000.

Quality Workbench© helps organizations keep day-to-day control over their quality systems in order to comply with ISO 9000 and QS-9000. It features document control, audits and nonconformities, customer complaints, and personnel training records.

Portspy Plus® allows you to transfer data easily from a wide variety of measuring devices into *SQCpack* for Windows and other popular software programs.

R&Rpack® utilizes the power of the personal computer to perform tedious repeatability and reproducibility studies with minimum effort.

DOEpack® is an effective software tool for setting up and analyzing experimental designs for all stages of production to find the optimal conditions in a process.

Total Quality Transformation® offers step-by-step help in facilitating the quality transformation in organizations. Materials include *Foundations for Leaders, Team Skills, Alignment Guide, Improvement Guide, Strategic Quality Planning Guide, Improvement Tools, Total Quality Tools*, and *Total Quality Tools* for Windows. *TQT* is a part of the Transformation of American Industry® training project which has been used in a variety of manufacturing and service organizations since 1984.

SPC Workout® is an interactive multimedia training course that provides effective step-by-step instruction on how to implement and use statistical process control. *SPC Workout*'s three modules—a statistics primer, control chart basics, and advanced control charting—make it suitable for workers at all levels. On-line exercises, and end-of-unit tests document the learners' progress while the colorful graphics and full audio keep learners interested.

Consulting and Training Services are offered by PQ Systems for companies at all stages of their quality management programs. A staff of highly-qualified consultants brings practical experience from both industrial and academic environments. Seminars and on-site training programs are available to help companies implement successful quality management programs.

INTRODUCTION

1. Purpose of this book

Our purpose in producing this book is to help people in health care to improve health care results by improving the systems and processes in which they work on a daily basis. Our hope is to do this by teaching quality improvement tools for:

- statistical process control

- identification of process flow variables, causes of variation, and ideas for improvement

By statistical process control, we mean identifying, constructing, and using the basic tools of **run charts, control charts, cause and effect diagram, histogram, Pareto chart, scatter diagram, and flow chart.** These are the key analytical tools that help identify causes of process variation, determine process stability and capability, predict the outcomes of processes, and plan for the future. It is our hope that the examples contained herein will illustrate some ideas for improvements in your workplace.

The Joint Commission on the Accreditation of Healthcare Organizations (JCAHO) and The National Committee on Quality Assurance (NCQA) in their most recently published standards move health care in the direction of:

- studying data over time

- moving from tables of numbers to graphical display of data

- measuring stability of important processes

- measuring stability of outcomes

- including statistical process control techniques in the data assessment process

This book is specifically designed to help each of you to meet these changing challenges!

2. WHAT THIS BOOK IS ABOUT—AND WHAT IT IS NOT ABOUT!

This book **does not** attempt to teach how to set up teams or provide prescriptive answers to specific health care problems. It **does** provide details as to how these tools are used in health care settings to make more sense out of data. The use of these tools will help improve operations at any level in a health care organization. Each tool has a specific health care example, and at the end of each chapter, a list of other uses for the tool is included.

3. OTHER HEALTH CARE ISSUES

Historically, statistical tools have been applied primarily to conducting health care research. Research involves the observation of an outcome under very controlled conditions and then making evaluations based on a set of controlled parameters. This method has been and continues to be very useful in the setting described. So naturally, when those in health care approach statistical tools for measurement of processes, they may think of statistics in research terms—chi, correlation coefficients, p values, and so forth.

The daily processes of health care delivery systems, at least the ones we've been part of, do not operate under precisely controlled conditions, however. The statistical tools most helpful in the improvement of daily health care delivery where factors are not tightly controlled, are not pure research methodologies, but are the types of tools in this book. The good news is that the tools in this book are easier for most of us to learn, share, and use in our everyday workplace. So let's get to work!

-Sandy & O.B. Murray

ATTRIBUTES CONTROL CHARTS: NONCONFORMING ITEMS

NP Control Charts

What is it?

An np-chart is an attributes control chart that shows how a system, measured by the **number** of nonconforming items produced, changes over time. The attribute (or characteristic) of interest is always in a yes/no, pass/fail, go/no-go form—for instance, the number of incomplete medical records in a constant daily, weekly, or monthly sample of 100. The number of patients discharged with Congestive Heart Failure (CHF) per 100 patients discharged, or the number of incomplete medical bills per 25 bills processed would also be charted on an np chart.

The purpose of this control chart (or **any** control chart) is to minimize the chance of making one of two mistakes when acting on a system: mistakes of overcontrol or undercontrol. The chart identifies the two types of variation present in a system, special and common, so the proper improvement action can be taken.

An np-chart is used to assess stability and to monitor improvement. Using the chart to assess stability first will determine what kind of action to plan next. Once the improvement action is implemented, we use the np-chart to monitor the system in order to see if the improvement action has worked.

~◯◯ WHAT DOES IT LOOK LIKE?

A completed example of an np-chart is shown below. A team made this chart to show the number of medical bills with mistakes. Each subgroup represents 100 medical bills.

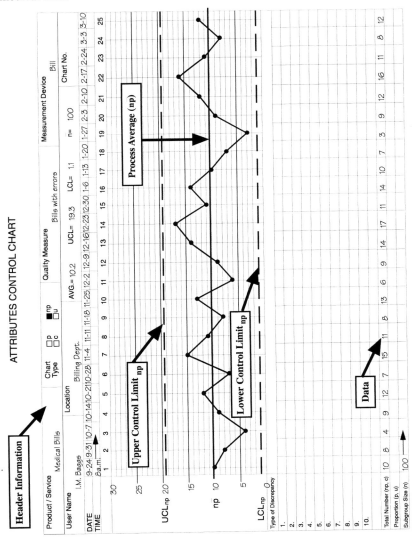

⊙ WHEN IS IT USED?

Use an np-chart when you can answer "yes" to all these questions:

1. **Do you need to assess system stability?** All control charts are used to assess stability of the system in order to minimize the chance of overcontrolling or undercontrolling the system.

2. **Is the data the number of nonconforming items per subgroup?** Usually this data comes from some inspection process whose aim is to judge whether a condition exists. Are invoices correct or not? Are medical records complete or not? Were patients readmitted or not? Did the patients die or live? Did the patients require treatment or not?

3. **Are all subgroups the same size?** An np-chart can only be used when all the subgroups are the same size. A p-chart could also be used in this situation.

4. **Are there only two outcomes to any given check?** Examples are defective or non defective, pass or fail, complete or incomplete. A c- or u-chart is used to chart the number of nonconformities, such as the number of defects or mistakes per subgroup or unit sampled. Some examples of this might be: Number of complications per subgroup of CABG patients, number of errors per medical record or subgroup of records, number of errors per patient bill or subgroup of patient bills.

5. **Has the characteristic being charted been operationally defined prior to data collection?** Operational definitions are important when collecting attributes data. Each data collector must have the same idea of what makes an item nonconforming so the results will be consistent. (See Operational Definitions.)

6. **Is the time order of subgroups preserved?** Since the control chart is designed to make it easy to study system changes over time, the order of subgroups is critical. Mixing the order of subgroups would be like developing movie film with the frames mixed. It would be like treating the patient, then doing an initial assessment, then getting his or her history—out of order!

4

⚒ How is it made?

These steps assume that the data has already been collected and the subgroup size is the same for all subgroups.

1. Complete the header information.

Fill in all the header information on the chart paper. The header information consists of product/service (e.g. medical bill, medical record, surgery, health assessment, laboratory test, home health visit), user name, chart type (in this case an np-chart), location (e.g. Pediatric Unit, Clinical Records, Surgery Department, Primary Care Clinic), quality measure, and measurement device. It is important that this information is completed so that others can understand the chart.

2. Record the data.

Record the data on the chart paper from the data collection sheet or directly on the chart paper as it is collected. Fill in the row marked "Total Number" with the number of occurrences (np) for each subgroup.

Also, fill in the row marked "Subgroup Size." Since it is constant for each subgroup, it is not necessary to write it in every box. Just write in the first box on the chart paper and draw an arrow indicating it is the same for all the subgroups. The example np-chart with completed header information and recorded data is shown below.

ATTRIBUTES CONTROL CHART

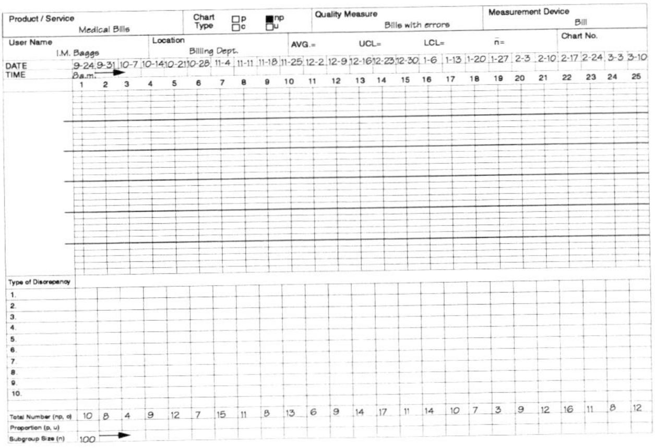

3. CALCULATE THE AVERAGE NUMBER.

The average number is known as $n\bar{p}$. It is found by adding the "Total Number" (np) row and dividing by the number of subgroups taken (k).

$$n\bar{p} = \frac{total\ number}{no.\ of\ subgroups}$$

$$= \frac{\Sigma np}{k}$$

For the example, $n\bar{p}$ is:

$$n\bar{p} = \frac{10 + 8 + 4 + \ldots + 12}{25}$$

$$= \frac{256}{25}$$

$$= 10.2$$

The value for $n\bar{p}$ should be carried out to one more decimal place than the np values have. Record $n\bar{p}$ in the space marked "AVG" at the top of the chart paper.

4. CALCULATE THE CONTROL LIMITS.

In order to assess the stability of the system, the control limits must be calculated. Control limits are lines drawn on the control chart that provide a basis for judging whether or not the system is stable. Twenty-five to thirty subgroups provide enough data to calculate control limits. If you decide to calculate limits with fewer subgroups, think of them as "trial" limits that should be recalculated after 25 subgroups have been collected.[1]

The formula for the upper control limit, UCL_{np}, is:

$$UCL_{np} = n\bar{p} + 3 \sqrt{n\bar{p}\,(1 - \frac{n\bar{p}}{n})}$$

UCL_{np} for the example is:

$$UCL_{np} = 10.2 + 3 \sqrt{10.2\,(1 - \frac{10.2}{100})}$$

$$= 10.2 + 3 \sqrt{10.2\,(.898)}$$

$$= 10.2 + 3(3.026)$$

$$= 19.3$$

---

[1] Donald J. Wheeler and David S. Chambers, *Understanding Statistical Process Control*, (Knoxville, TN: Statistical Process Controls, Inc., 1986), p. 79.

The formula for the lower control limit, LCL_{np}, is:

$$LCL_{np} = n\bar{p} - 3 \sqrt{n\bar{p} \left(1 - \frac{n\bar{p}}{n}\right)}$$

LCL_{np} for the example is:

$$LCL_{np} = 10.2 - 3 \sqrt{10.2 \left(1 - \frac{10.2}{100}\right)}$$

$$= 10.2 - 3 \sqrt{10.2 \, (.898)}$$

$$= 10.2 - 3(3.026)$$

$$= 1.1$$

The control limits should be recorded to one more decimal place than the np values have. Record the values for the control limits in the spaces marked "UCL" and "LCL" at the top of the chart.

5. DETERMINE THE SCALING FOR THE CHART.

Scaling means numbering the lines along the left of the chart so the points can be plotted. Scaling can be the most difficult part of constructing a control chart. When following the steps for scaling, be careful not to get caught up in trying to make the calculations perfect. The important consideration is that the chart is readable and easy to make.

Begin by finding the largest np (number) value from the data entry section of the chart. Compare this value to the upper control limit and write down the larger of the two. In the example, the largest np value is 17 and the upper control limit is 19.3, so write down 19.3.

Next, divide the number you have written by about two-thirds of the total number of lines on the np-chart. Use only two-thirds of the available lines in order to leave space outside the control limits to plot shifts in the future. The result of the division is the increment value for each line on the control chart.

The number you have recorded is 19.3. There are 30 lines on the chart paper, so use 20 (two-thirds) to make the chart.

The increment value is: $\dfrac{19.3}{20} = .97$

The increment value should be rounded upward as necessary so the dark reference lines (usually every fifth line) can be labeled with an easy-to-work-with number such as a multiple of 1, 2, 5, 10. Round .97 to 1 for easier numbering.

To number (scale) the lines, start at the bottom line (labeled 0) of the chart and add the increment value (1 in this case) to each line as you move upward on the chart. Label each dark reference line with its value.

For the example, starting at the bottom line (labeled 0) each dark reference line is labeled 5, 10, 15, 20, 25, and 30. The example completed through this step is shown below.

ATTRIBUTES CONTROL CHART

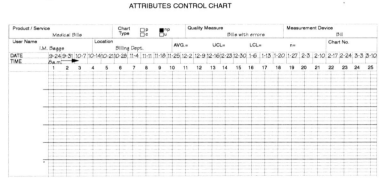

6. **DRAW THE CENTERLINE AND CONTROL LIMITS.**

Draw a dark horizontal line on the chart to represent $n\bar{p}$. Draw dark dashed horizontal lines to represent the upper and lower control limits for the chart. Label each line with the appropriate label ($n\bar{p}$, UCL_{np}, LCL_{np}). The example completed through this step is shown below.

ATTRIBUTES CONTROL CHART

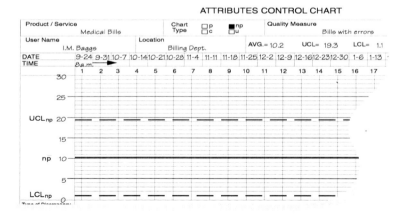

7. PLOT THE VALUES ON THE CHART.

Plot the np values for each subgroup on the chart. Connect the dots with straight lines. The completed example is shown below.

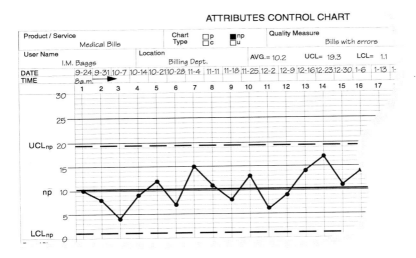

ATTRIBUTES CONTROL CHART

Product / Service		Chart Type	☐p ☐c	■np ☐u	Quality Measure		
Medical Bills					Bills with errors		
User Name	Location						
I.M. Baggs	Billing Dept.			AVG.= 10.2	UCL= 19.3	LCL= 1.1

DATE: 9-24 9-31 10-7 10-14 10-21 10-28 11-4 11-11 11-18 11-25 12-2 12-9 12-16 12-23 12-30 1-6 1-13 1-
TIME: 8a.m.

8. INTERPRET THE CONTROL CHART.

The np-chart is interpreted by using the same rules used for all control charts. (See "Chart Interpretation" for further discussion.) The basic rules for interpreting out-of-control conditions are listed below.

1. Any point lying outside the control limits.

2. Run of seven points:

   a. seven or more points in a row above or below the centerline
   b. seven or more points in a row going in one direction, up or down

3. Any nonrandom pattern, including the following typical cases:

   a. too close to the average
   b. too far from the average
   c. cycles

The example np-chart shows that the medical billing system is stable. No out-of-control conditions exist. The system can be improved only by reducing common causes of variation in the invoicing process.

When systems are declared to be stable, the control limits calculated previously are simply drawn onto new chart paper as subgroups continue to be collected. This will allow the user to make decisions about the system's stability as each new subgroup is plotted. New control limits are calculated only when a change is made to the system.

REMEMBER

1. An np-chart records the number of nonconforming items per subgroup.

2. The subgroups must all be the same size to use an np-chart.

3. The characteristics being studied, such as incomplete medical records, an incorrect invoice, a treatment that failed, or an unplanned readmission, are considered defective items, and must be operationally defined prior to data collection.

GETTING THE MOST FROM NP-CHARTS

Getting the most from control charts means being able to use them for several different purposes as you make improvements in the system.

When beginning to work on system improvement, **assess stability** of the system. The purpose of assessing stability is to analyze the factors which contribute to variability. Pick an important quality characteristic of process output (clinical outcome, cost outcome, satisfaction outcome, etc.) and track it over time with a control chart. In a health care process, these characteristics are often inspection data on the number of defective outcomes per constant sample size. The characteristic might be the number of medical bills with missing information from a constant sample size or the number of surgical patients experiencing a complication from a constant sample size. In a service or administrative process, such a characteristic might be the number of insurance claims with missing information from a constant sample size. Many factors influence the overall variability of a system, but until this first chart is made, one does not know whether to begin to work on common or special causes.

Once system stability is assessed, pay special attention to the need to **stratify data.** Sometimes you will find sources of variability this way. There may be fewer medical bills with errors from a particular clinic, nursing unit, or a service. You may find that one billing clerk or one billing operation within the system has consistently more correct bills than others. You must select your subgroups and record your data in a way that allows you to stratify the outcome by time, location, type, demographic, shift, DRG, or other logical categories. The actual check may be as simple as regrouping the np-chart subgroups.

To **generate improvement theories,** move your investigation upstream in the process to focus on the resources or variables that contribute to variability. They may be the causes identified on your cause-and-effect diagram. Often you may need to apply control charts to the process or causal variables to tell whether they are stable. Reduce the variability or number of defectives in each of these factors, and you will reduce the overall system variability and failure rate. Suppose you discover that Hospital A is using a computerized screening program to check applicable codes on the billing record before it is submitted, while the other hospitals in your system use a manual system. This method may account for the difference between Hospital A and the other hospitals in the system in the number of accurate bills you observe. Standardize the improvement and test it at another hospital in the system and continue to track the number of incomplete forms. The control chart used in this way will help you decide if the method really makes a difference and whether the billing system has been improved. If so, you could replicate the improvement in the other hospitals, continuing to track the number of correct bills per 100 to determine if the change was really an improvement.

The question of when to calculate new control limits always arises here. Should you **calculate new limits** when you standardize and replicate the Hospital A method throughout the system? Yes! But wait until you see statistical evidence that the change has had an impact on your variable, such as a system shift or other out-of-control evidence. (Note: when recalculating control limits after a system change, use only those subgroups collected since the change occurred.) In general, once control limits are calculated, they are simply projected onto new forms as additional data is gathered, so the operator has an ongoing way to assess stability as soon as a new subgroup is gathered and recorded. When you make a system change, you must write it on the chart. This way you can identify exactly which points on the chart correspond to the new method—and begin with those when you recalculate limits.

Finally, using the control chart for **standardization** means maintaining data collection and responding to special causes. Imagine that you had studied the number of complete bills over six months, made changes to standardize methods, and immediately stopped collecting data. What would happen? First, you would have only perception and opinion to tell you whether you had made improvements by your action. More importantly, you would have no way to identify unusual sources of variability that may crop up as the billing departments continue to process bills. Perhaps the offices will begin to process bills for home health services as well as inpatient services. Without a control chart, there is no way to know if the system has changed. Special causes will appear and you can detect them only when you have the statistical knowledge to recognize them.

Using the control chart for standardization suggests a system that has been well defined. The system is one whose variables are understood and whose most important procedures and elements are standardized. In other words, stable, predictable processes are more likely to result when standards of operation are in place and executed routinely. Clearly, one expects that standards and methods will change as improvements are discovered, but it becomes the responsibility of the manager to communicate such changes to all concerned in order to minimize the variability which is inevitable in even the most well-controlled systems.

In most organizations, data is quite readily available in attribute form. As you refine your study of variation and move upstream in processes, you may find that you have a greater need for variables data.

 ## OTHER HEALTH CARE EXAMPLES:

- Number of incorrect medical bills per subgroup of 25 bills

- Number of incomplete medical records per 20 medical records

- Number of patients who are "no shows" per 1000 clinic appointments

- Number of substance abuse outpatients who fail to complete the program per 25 who began the program

- Number of post CABG patients who experience a complication per 20 CABG patients

- Number of inpatients who fall per 100 inpatients admitted

- Number of HMO participants who fail to re-enroll per 1000 eligible to reenroll

WHAT IS IT?

A p-chart is an attributes control chart that shows how a system, measured by the **proportion** of nonconforming items produced, changes over time. For this chart, the attribute (or characteristic) being charted is always in a yes/no form. Other examples of this form are conforming/nonconforming, nondefective/ defective, complete/incomplete, go/no-go, and pass/fail. In health care, the proportion of: incomplete medical records, treatments that didn't work, incomplete medical bills, or inpatient deaths would be charted on a p-chart. A p-chart can be used for equal or unequal subgroup sizes.

The purpose of this control chart (or any control chart) is to minimize the chance of making one of two mistakes when acting on a system: mistakes of overcontrol or undercontrol. The chart identifies the two types of variation present in a system, special and common, so the proper improvement action can be taken.

A p-chart is used by teams to assess process and outcome stability. When assessing stability, we are trying to determine which causes of variation are present in the system. Only then will we know which actions will be appropriate to improve the system, which actions will eliminate special causes, or which actions will reduce common causes of variation.

After an improvement action has been implemented, we use a p-chart to study the results of the improvement action. That is, we use it to monitor the improvement over time. The goal is to reduce the number of nonconforming items produced by the system.

👓 WHAT DOES IT LOOK LIKE?

Shown below is an example of a p-chart in which the subgroup size is constant. An improvement team made this chart to show the proportion of medical bills with mistakes. Each subgroup represents 100 medical bills.

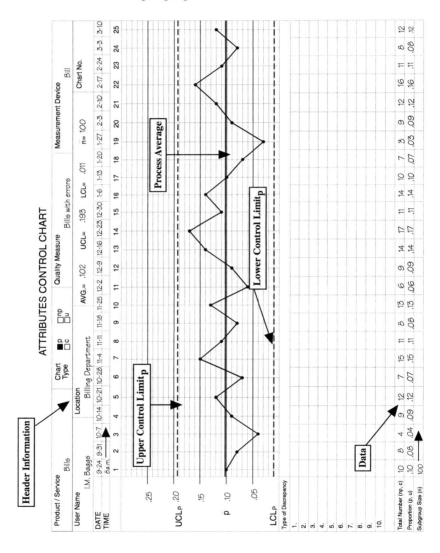

⊙ WHEN IS IT USED?

Use a p-chart when you can answer "yes" to all these questions:

1. **Do you need to assess system stability?** All control charts are used to assess stability of the system in order to minimize the chance of overcontrolling or undercontrolling the system.

2. **Does the data consist of counts that can be converted to proportions?** Usually this data comes from some inspection process whose aim is to judge whether a condition exists. Are results good or bad? Are medical bills correct or not? Was physical therapy a success or not?

3. **Are there only two outcomes to any given check?** Examples are defective or nondefective, pass or fail, complete or incomplete. A c- or u-chart is used to chart the number of nonconformities, such as the number of defects or mistakes per subgroup or unit sampled. Some examples of this might be number of complications per subgroup of CABG patients, number of errors per medical record or subgroup of records, number of errors per patient bill or subgroup of patient bills.

4. **Has the characteristic being charted been operationally defined prior to data collection?** Operational definitions are particularly important when collecting attributes data. Each data collector must have the same idea of what makes an item nonconforming so the results will be consistent. (See Operational Definitions.)

5. **Is the time order of subgroups preserved?** Since the control chart is designed to make it easy to study system changes over time, the order of subgroups is critical. Mixing the order of subgroups would be like developing movie film with the frames mixed. It would be like treating the patient, then doing an initial assessment, then getting his or her history—out of order!

 How is it made?

These steps assume the data has already been collected.

1. Complete the header information.

Fill in all the header information on the chart paper. The header information consists of product/service, user name, chart type (in this case a p-chart), location, quality measure, and measurement device. It is important that this information is completed so that others who may look at the chart can understand it.

2. Record the data.

Record the data on the chart paper from the data collection sheet or directly on the chart as it is collected. Fill in the boxes marked "Subgroup Size" and "Total Number." The "Total Number" row refers to the number of occurrences (passes or fails depending on which you intend to track), known as np, in each subgroup.

3. Calculate the proportion for each subgroup.

Calculate the proportion of occurrence for each subgroup on the chart. The proportion (p) is found by dividing the total number (np) by the subgroup size (n). In the example, the total number in the first subgroup is 10 and the subgroup size is 100. Therefore, the proportion (p) is:

$$p_1 = \frac{np}{n}$$
$$= \frac{10}{100}$$
$$= .10$$

The total number in the second subgroup is 8 and the subgroup size is 100, so the proportion (p) is:

$$p_2 = \frac{np}{n}$$
$$= \frac{8}{100}$$
$$= .08$$

Generally, p values should be carried out to two decimal places.

16

4. CALCULATE THE AVERAGE PROPORTION.

The average proportion ($\bar{p}$) is found by adding the "Total Number" (np) row and dividing by the total number checked (total of the "Subgroup Size" row).

In the example, the total number for all the subgroups is 256 and the total number checked is 2,500. So $\bar{p}$ is:

$$\bar{p} = \frac{total\ number}{total\ no.\ checked}$$

$$= \frac{\Sigma np}{\Sigma n}$$

$$= \frac{256}{2,500}$$

$$= .102$$

$$\bar{n} = Average\ Sample\ Size$$

$$\bar{n} = 100$$

Record $\bar{p}$ to one decimal place more than the p values contain. Write $\bar{p}$ in the space marked "AVG" at the top of the chart.

Caution: Trying to calculate $\bar{p}$ by adding the subgroup proportions (p) and dividing by the number of subgroups is incorrect.

5. CALCULATE THE CONTROL LIMITS.

In order to assess the stability of the system, the control limits must be calculated. Control limits are lines drawn on the control chart which provide a basis for judging whether or not the system is stable. Twenty-five to thirty subgroups are enough data to calculate control limits. If you decide to calculate limits with fewer subgroups, think of them as "trial" limits that should be recalculated after 25 subgroups have been collected.[1]

---

[1] Donald J. Wheeler and David S. Chambers, *Understanding Statistical Process Control* (Knoxville, TN: Statistical Process Controls, Inc., 1986), p. 79.

The formula for the upper control limit, UCL_p, is:

$$UCL_p = \bar{p} + 3 \sqrt{\frac{\bar{p}\,(1 - \bar{p})}{\bar{n}}}$$

UCL_p for the example is:

$$UCL_p = .102 + 3 \sqrt{\frac{.102(1 - .102)}{100}}$$

$$= .102 + 3 \sqrt{.000915960}$$

$$= .102 + 3\,(.0302638)$$

$$= .1928$$

The formula for the lower control limit, LCL_p, is:

$$LCL_p = \bar{p} - 3 \sqrt{\frac{\bar{p}(1 - \bar{p})}{\bar{n}}}$$

LCL_p for the example is:

$$LCL_p = .102 - 3 \sqrt{\frac{.102(1 - .102)}{100}}$$

$$= .102 - 3 \sqrt{.000915960}$$

$$= .102 - 3\,(.0302638)$$

$$= .0112$$

Record the values for the control limits in the spaces marked "UCL" and "LCL" at the top of the chart.

6. DETERMINE THE SCALING FOR THE CHART.

The p-chart is scaled in the same manner as the np-chart. Remember that the increment value should be rounded so the dark reference lines can be labeled with an easy-to-work-with number such as a multiple of 1, 2, 5, 10, etc. (See Step 5 in the np-chart section for details on scaling.)

18

7. DRAW THE CENTERLINE AND CONTROL LIMITS.

Draw a dark horizontal line to represent $\bar{p}$ on the chart. Draw dark dashed horizontal lines to represent each control limit on the chart. Label each line ($\bar{p}$, UCL_p, LCL_p).

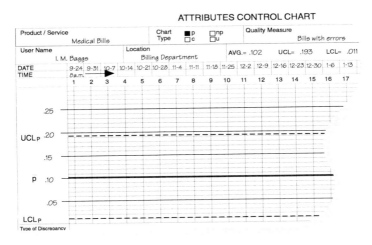

8. PLOT THE VALUES ON THE CHART.

Plot a point on the chart for each p value from each subgroup. Connect the dots with straight lines. The completed example is shown below.

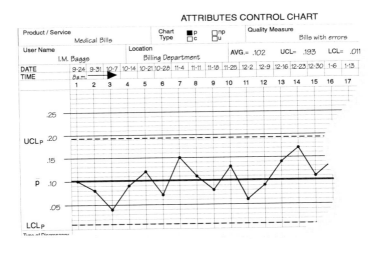

9. INTERPRET THE CONTROL CHART.

The p-chart can be interpreted using the same rules used for other control charts. (See Chart Interpretation for more discussion on chart interpretation.) The basic rules for interpreting out-of-control conditions are listed below.

1. Any point lying outside the control limits.

2. Run of seven points:

    a. seven or more points in a row above or below the centerline
    b. seven or more points in a row going in one direction, up or down

3. Any nonrandom pattern, including the following typical cases:

    a. too close to the average
    b. too far from the average
    c. cycles

The example p-chart shows that the medical billing system is stable. No out-of-control conditions exist. The system can be improved only by reducing common causes of variation in the invoicing process.

When systems have been declared to be stable, the control limits calculated previously are simply drawn onto new chart paper as subgroups continue to be collected. This method will allow the user to make decisions about the system's stability as each new subgroup is plotted. New control limits are calculated only when a change is made to the system.

 OTHER HEALTH CARE EXAMPLES:

• Proportion of customers rating us fair or lower per 50 returned surveys

• Proportion of patients with a repeat C-section per subgroup of 50 initial C-section deliveries

• Proportion of deaths per 1000 patients admitted

• Proportion of outpatient clinic patients who are "no shows" per 100 appointments

 **VARIATIONS**

In some circumstances, the size of the subgroup varies. If the subgroup size varies by more than 25 percent, the procedure described in the following section should be used.

P CONTROL CHART VARIABLE SAMPLE SIZE

 WHAT IS IT?

A p-chart is an attributes control chart that shows how a system, measured by the **proportion** of nonconforming items produced, changes over time. For this chart, the attribute (or characteristic) being charted is always in a yes/no form. Other examples of this form are conforming/nonconforming, nondefective/defective, complete/incomplete, go/no-go and pass/fail. In health care the proportion of incomplete medical records per month, patients developing a complication per week, incomplete medical bills per week, and patient deaths per monthly admission would be charted on an np-chart.

The purpose of this control chart (or any control chart) is to minimize the chance of making one of two mistakes when acting on a system: mistakes of overcontrol or undercontrol. The chart identifies the two types of variation present in a system, special and common, so the proper improvement action can be taken.

A p-chart is used to assess stability and to study results. When assessing stability we are trying to determine which causes of variation are present in the system. Only then will we know which actions will be appropriate to improve the system, which actions will eliminate special causes, or which actions will reduce common causes of variation.

After an improvement action has been implemented, a p-chart is used to study the results of the improvement action. That is, the user uses it to monitor the improvement over time. The goal is to reduce the number of nonconforming items produced by the system.

⟋◯◯ WHAT DOES IT LOOK LIKE?

An example of a p-chart with variable subgroup size is shown below. Notice
that the control limits change for some subgroups. These subgroups vary in size
by more than 25 percent from the average subgroup. This chart shows the
proportion of liveborn infants with birth weight of less than 2500 grams born to
mothers identified as "high risk" in a major medical system.

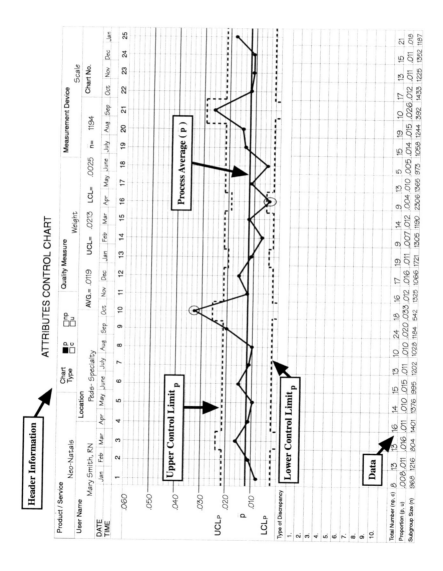

22

⊘ WHEN IS IT USED?

NOTE: A p-chart can handle constant or variable subgroup size. However, if subgroups vary by more than 25 percent from the average subgroup size, special calculations are required. If the subgroup size is constant, an np-chart can also be used. The np-chart is somewhat simpler and may, therefore, be more desirable for a constant subgroup size.

Use a p-chart when you can answer "yes" to all these questions:

1. **Do you need to assess system stability?** All control charts are used to assess stability of the system in order to minimize the chance of overcontrolling or undercontrolling the system.

2. **Does the data consist of counts that can be converted to proportions?** Usually this data comes from some inspection process whose aim is to judge whether a condition exists. Are results good or bad? Are invoices correct or not? Did the patient live or die? Was the surgery complication free or not? Are diagnostic forms complete or not? Are medical records complete or not?

3. **Can there be only two outcomes to any given check?** Examples are, defective or nondefective, pass or fail, complete or incomplete. A c- or u-chart is used to chart the number of nonconformities such as the number of defects or mistakes per subgroup or unit sampled with a c- or u- chart. The assumption is that each unit or subgroup could have multiple errors or defects. Some examples of this might be number of complications per subgroup of CABG patients, number of errors per medical record or subgroup of records, number of errors per patient bill or subgroup of patient bills.

4. **Has the characteristic being charted been operationally defined prior to data collection?** Operational definitions are particularly important when collecting attributes data. Each data collector must have the same idea of what makes an item nonconforming so the results will be consistent. (See Operational Definitions.)

5. **Is the time order of subgroups preserved?** Since the control chart is designed to make it easy to study system changes over time, the order of subgroups is critical. Mixing the order of subgroups would be like developing movie film with the frames mixed. It would be like treating the patient, then doing an initial assessment, then getting his or her history—out of order!

How is it Made?

These steps assume the data has already been collected.

1. Complete the header information.

Fill in all the header information on the chart paper. The header information consists of product/service, user name, chart type (in this case a p-chart), location, quality measure, and measurement device. It is important that this information is completed so that others who may look at the chart can understand it.

2. Record the data.

Record the data on the chart paper from the data collection sheet or directly on the chart as it is collected. Fill in the boxes marked "Subgroup Size" and "Total Number." The "Total Number" row refers to the number of occurrences, known as np, in each subgroup.

3. Calculate the proportion for each subgroup.

Calculate the proportion of occurrence for each subgroup on the chart. The proportion (p) is found by dividing the total number (np) by the subgroup size (n). In the example, the total number in the first subgroup is 8 and the subgroup size is 968. Therefore, the proportion (p) is:

$$p_1 = \frac{np}{n}$$

$$= \frac{8}{968}$$

$$= .008$$

24

The total number in the second subgroup is 13 and the subgroup size is 1216, so the proportion (p) is:

$$p_2 = \frac{np}{n}$$

$$= \frac{13}{1216}$$

$$= .011$$

Generally, p values should be carried out to three decimal places.

4. CALCULATE THE AVERAGE PROPORTION.

The average proportion ($\bar{p}$) is found by adding the "Total Number" (np) row and dividing by the total number checked (total of the "Subgroup Size" row).

In the example, the total number for all the subgroups is 356 and the total number checked is 29,858. So $\bar{p}$ is:

$$\bar{p} = \frac{total\ number}{total\ no.\ checked}$$

$$= \frac{\sum np}{\sum n}$$

$$= \frac{356}{29,858}$$

$$= .0119$$

Record $\bar{p}$ to one decimal place more than the p values contain. Write $\bar{p}$ in the space marked "AVG" at the top of the chart.

Caution: Trying to calculate $\bar{p}$ by adding the subgroup proportions (p) and dividing by the number of subgroups is incorrect.

5. CALCULATE THE CONTROL LIMITS.

a. Calculate the average subgroup size.

The subgroup size ($\bar{n}$) is found by adding the total number checked (total of the "Subgroup Size" row) by the number of subgroups taken (k). In the example shown under "What does it look like?" the total number checked is 29,858 and there are 25 subgroups, so $\bar{n}$ is:

$$\bar{n} = \frac{\Sigma n}{k}$$

$$= \frac{29,858}{25}$$

$$= 1194$$

b. Determine the subgroup size limits.

The easiest approach to the problem of variable subgroup size is to calculate the values for 25 percent above and below the average subgroup size ($\bar{n}$) before calculating control limits. Then each subgroup size can be compared to these two numbers to determine where control limits must be recalculated.

In the example, $\bar{n}$ is 1194. To determine the 25 percent above and below values, multiply 1194 by 1.25 and .75.

Use these subgroup size limits to identify subgroups whose limits vary excessively. In the example, subgroups 3, 10, 13, 16, and 21 fall outside these subgroup boundaries.

c. Calculate the control limits for all the data.

Calculate the control limits using all the subgroups (even if you identified subgroups in Step 5b). These will be the control limits for the subgroups whose size does not vary by more than 25 percent from $\bar{n}$. Use $\bar{n}$ for n in the formulas for control limits.

The formula for the upper control limit, UCL_p, is:

$$UCL_p = \bar{p} + 3\sqrt{\frac{\bar{p}\,(1-\bar{p})}{\bar{n}}}$$

26

UCL_p for the example is:

$$UCL_p = .0119 + 3 \sqrt{\frac{.0119(1 - .0119)}{1194}}$$

$$= .0119 + 3 \sqrt{.0000098}$$

$$= .0213$$

The formula for the lower control limit, LCL_p, is:

$$LCL_p = \bar{p} - 3 \sqrt{\frac{\bar{p}(1 - \bar{p})}{\bar{n}}}$$

LCL_p for the example is:

$$LCL_p = .0119 - 3 \sqrt{\frac{.0119(1 - .0119)}{1194}}$$

$$= .0119 - 3 \sqrt{.0000098}$$

$$= .0025$$

These will be the upper and lower control limits for most of the subgroups on the chart. Those subgroups identified in Step 5b as varying excessively will have separate control limits. If no subgroups were identified in Step 5b, you are finished with control limit calculations.

d. Calculate the control limits for subgroups that vary excessively.

In Step 5b, you identified five subgroups that are outside the subgroup size limits—subgroups 3, 10, 13, 16, and 21. Separate control limits must be calculated for each of the five subgroups.

Subgroup 3, taken in March, has a subgroup size of 804, which is below the allowed 896. So, the control limits must be recalculated for this subgroup, using its size of 804 for n in the formula.

The control limits for subgroup 3 are as follows:

$$UCL_{k=3} = .0119 + 3 \sqrt{\frac{.0119(1 - .0119)}{804}}$$

$$= .0119 + 3 \sqrt{.0000146}$$

$$= .0234$$

$$LCL_{k=3} = .0119 - 3 \sqrt{\frac{.0119(1 - .0119)}{804}}$$

$$= .0119 - 3 \sqrt{.0000146}$$

$$= .0004$$

Continue calculations for the remaining subgroups (10, 13, 16, 21). Notice that if the subgroup size varies below $\bar{n}$ by more than 25 percent, the control limits will be wider for that subgroup. And if the subgroup size varies above $\bar{n}$ by more than 25 percent, the control limits will become more narrow. A bigger subgroup size narrows the control limits.

6. DETERMINE THE SCALING FOR THE CHART.

The p-chart is scaled in the same manner as the np-chart. Remember that the increment value should be rounded so the dark reference lines can be labeled with an easy-to-work-with number such as a multiple of 1, 2, 5, 10 etc. (See Step 5 in the np-chart section for details on scaling.)

7. DRAW THE CENTERLINE AND CONTROL LIMITS.

Draw a dark horizontal line to represent $\bar{p}$ on the chart. Draw dark dashed horizontal lines to represent each control limit on the chart. Label each line ($\bar{p}$, UCL_p, LCL_p). Remember to draw in variable control limits for the subgroups that vary excessively in size.

8. PLOT THE VALUES ON THE CHART.

Plot a point on the chart for each p value from each subgroup. Connect the dots with straight lines.

9. INTERPRET THE CONTROL CHART.

The p-chart can be interpreted using the same rules used for other control charts. (See Chart Interpretation for more discussion on chart interpretation.) The basic rules for interpreting out-of-control conditions are listed below.

1. Any point lying outside the control limits.

2. Run of seven points:

   a. seven or more points in a row above or below the centerline
   b. seven or more points in a row going in one direction, up or down

3. Any nonrandom pattern, including the following typical cases:

   a. too close to the average
   b. too far from the average
   c. cycles

The example p-chart shows two points outside the control limits (subgroups 10 and 16). This indicates that special causes of system variation are present and should be investigated. In this case, the clinical team discovered that the special cause for subgroup 10 was related to multiple births inducing premature delivery in some high risk mothers. In this case, the special cause should be noted, since it is outside of the ability of the clinical team to correct, but may occur from time to time. When special causes are discovered, they should be written on the chart next to the point.

The special cause in subgroup 16 is still being investigated.

When systems are declared to be stable, the control limits calculated previously are simply drawn onto new chart paper as subgroups continue to be collected. This will allow the process owner, or in this case the clinical team, to make decisions about the system's stability as each new subgroup is plotted. New control limits are calculated only when a change is made to the system.

 ## OTHER HEALTH CARE EXAMPLES:

- Proportion of repeat lab tests per total tests done per week

- Proportion of deaths per total number of inpatients admitted per month

- Proportion of patients returning for scheduled follow-up per number directed to follow up each month

- Proportion of those dropping out of mental health therapy within a month of beginning per total number who began therapy

- Proportion of ASA level three or higher surgical patients per number of surgeries performed per month

- Proportion of inpatients who fell per number admitted per month

- Proportion of HMO enrollees not re-enrolling per number eligible to re-enroll per month

ATTRIBUTES CONTROL CHARTS: NONCONFORMITIES

 **What is it?**

A c-chart is an attributes control chart used to monitor a system, measured by the number of nonconformities per subgroup the system produces. Nonconformities are defects or occurrences found in the sampled subgroup. A missing signature, a missing document, a complication, and a mistake can all be considered nonconformities. Any characteristic present that should not be, or any characteristic not present that should be can be considered a nonconformity.

The purpose of this control chart (or any control chart) is to minimize the chance of making one of two mistakes when acting on a system: mistakes of overcontrol or undercontrol. The chart identifies the two types of variation present in a system, special and common, so the proper improvement action can be taken.

C-charts are particularly useful in situations where the item is too complex to be ruled as simply entirely conforming or nonconforming (pass/fail). In a health care setting, a medical record might have several discrepancies but as a whole the record is usable—it passes. The outcome of an outpatient visit, procedure, or surgery may be good or bad (pass /fail) but defects in the delivery of the care can exist, such as mistakes in medications, or a laceration. In this case, a c-chart would be useful to record the number of defects in a constant number of procedures, visits, or surgeries.

We would use a c-chart to assess the stability of the system which it is trying to improve and to study results. Once the stability of the system is known, we can plan the correct improvement action. Then we can continue gathering data for the c-chart to see if the improvement action has worked.

∽ 👓 WHAT DOES IT LOOK LIKE?

An example of a completed c-chart is shown below. This c-chart was made by a team to assess the stability of a system producing medical records with discrepancies. A subgroup size of one clinical record was sampled five times per day.

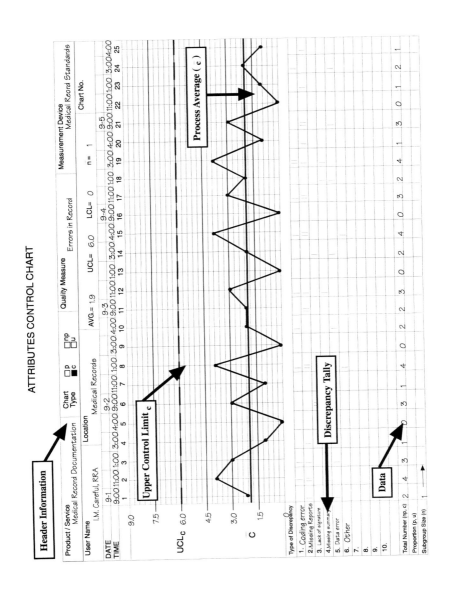

 WHEN IS IT USED?

Use a c-chart when you can answer "yes" to all these questions:

1. **Do you need to assess system stability?** All control charts are used to assess stability of the system in order to minimize the chance of overcontrolling or undercontrolling the system.

2. **Does the data represent the number of nonconformities per subgroup?** Examples include the number of defects or mistakes. A medical bill, record, appointment form, procedure or treatment might have several errors. This is attributes data or counts. If you were counting an entire item as defective or nonconforming (pass/fail), you would use a p- or np-chart.

3. **Is the subgroup size the same for all subgroups?** If the subgroup size is the same for all subgroups, a c- or u-chart can be used. (A c-chart reflects the number of discrepancies per a single medical bill or the number of discrepancies per 5 medical records.) If the subgroups are different sizes and you are charting the number of nonconformities, a u-chart would be used. A u-chart represents number of discrepancies per day's charts (number of charts produced would vary from day to day), number of discrepancies per hour's prescriptions or laboratory tests (the number of scripts or laboratory tests will vary from hour to hour).

4. **Have the possible nonconformities been operationally defined prior to data collection?** Operational definitions are especially important when collecting attributes data. The characteristic being charted should be operationally defined prior to collection. This is to insure that each data collector has the same idea of what the characteristic is and how to collect it so the results will be consistent. (See Operational Definitions.)

5. **Is the time order of the subgroups preserved?** Since the control chart is designed to make it easy to study system changes over time, the order of subgroups is critical. Mixing the order of subgroups would be like developing movie film with the frames mixed. It would be like treating the patient, then doing an initial assessment, then getting his or her history— out of order!

HOW IS IT MADE?

These steps assume that the data has already been collected and recorded on a data collection sheet or on the control chart paper.

1. COMPLETE THE HEADER INFORMATION.

Fill in all the header information at the top of the chart. The header information consists of product/service, user name, location, quality measure, measurement device, and type of chart (in this case a c-chart). It is important to complete this information so that anyone who reads the chart can understand it.

2. RECORD THE DATA.

Record the data on the chart paper from the data collection sheet, or as it is being collected. Fill in the rows marked "Total Number" and "Subgroup Size." The "Total Number" row refers to the number of nonconformities, called c, such as defects or errors per subgroup. Since the subgroup size is the same for all subgroups on a c-chart, fill in the first box on the "Subgroup Size" row and draw an arrow indicating repetition.

The attributes control chart paper has a section labeled "Type of Discrepancy." This section is for listing the types of defects or errors found in each subgroup. Notes regarding process changes and observations are also helpful here. This will help later when the causes for nonconformities are being investigated. The example c-chart with completed header information and recorded data is shown below.

ATTRIBUTES CONTROL CHART

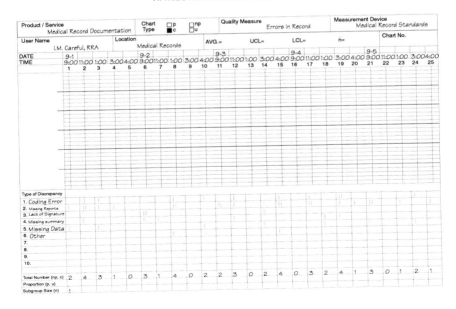

3. CALCULATE THE AVERAGE NUMBER.

The average number is found by adding the "Total Number" (c) row and dividing by the number of subgroups taken (k).

$$\bar{c} = \frac{total\ number}{no.\ of\ subgroups}$$

$$= \frac{\sum c}{k}$$

$$= \frac{c_1 + c_2 + c_3 + \ldots + c_k}{k}$$

In the example, $\bar{c}$ is:

$$\bar{c} = \frac{2 + 4 + 3 + \ldots + 1}{25}$$

$$= \frac{48}{25}$$

$$= 1.9$$

The value found for $\bar{c}$ should be recorded to one decimal place more than the c values. Record the value for $\bar{c}$ in the space marked "AVG" at the top of the chart.

4. CALCULATE THE CONTROL LIMITS.

In order to assess the stability of the system, the control limits must be calculated. Control limits are lines drawn on the control chart used as a basis for judging whether or not the system is stable. Twenty-five to 30 subgroups provide enough data to calculate control limits. If you decide to calculate limits with fewer subgroups, think of them as "trial" limits that should be recalculated after 25 subgroups have been collected.[1]

The formula for the upper control limit, UCL_c, is:

$$UCL_c = \bar{c} + 3\sqrt{\bar{c}}$$

---

[1] Donald J. Wheeler and David S. Chambers, *Understanding Statistical Process Control*, (Knoxville, TN: Statistical Process Controls, Inc., 1986), p. 79.

In the example UCL_c is:

$$UCL_C = 1.9 + 3\sqrt{1.9}$$

$$= 1.9 + 4.1$$

$$= 6.0$$

The formula for the lower control limits, LCL_c, is:

$$LCL_C = \bar{c} - 3\sqrt{\bar{c}}$$

In the example LCL_c is:

$$LCL_C = 1.9 - 3\sqrt{1.9}$$

$$= -2.2$$

$$\approx 0$$

In this case, round LCL_c to 0 because a negative defect does not make sense. Both control limits are recorded to one decimal place more than c values. Record the values found for the upper and lower control limits in the spaces provided at the top of the chart marked UCL and LCL.

5. DETERMINE THE SCALING FOR THE CHART.

Scaling means numbering the lines along the left of the chart so the points can be plotted. Scaling can be the most difficult and inexact part of constructing a control chart. When following the steps for scaling, be careful not to get caught up in trying to make the calculations perfect. The important thing is that the chart is readable and easy to make.

Begin by finding the largest c (number) from the data entry section of the chart. Compare this value to the upper control limit and write down the larger of the two. In the example, the largest c value is 4 and the upper control limit is 6.0. Therefore, write down 6.0.

Next, divide this number by about two-thirds of the total number of lines on the c-chart. Use two-thirds of the available lines in order to leave space outside the control limits to plot shifts in the future. The result of the division is the increment value for each line on the control chart.

The number written down is 6.0. The chart paper has 30 lines, so use 20 (two-thirds) to make the chart.

The increment value is: $\dfrac{6.0}{20} = .3$

The increment value should be rounded upward as necessary so the dark reference lines (usually every fifth line) can be labeled with an easy-to-work-with number such as a multiple of 1, 2, 5, 10, etc. Since the increment value (.3) will allow you to label every fifth line in increments of 1.5, keep .3.

To number (scale) the lines, start at the bottom line (labeled 0) on the chart and add the increment value (.3 in this case) to each line as you move upward on the chart. Label each dark reference line with its value.

In the example, starting at the bottom line (labeled 0), each dark reference line is labeled 1.5, 3.0, 4.5, 6.0, 7.5, and 9.0. The example completed through this step is shown below.

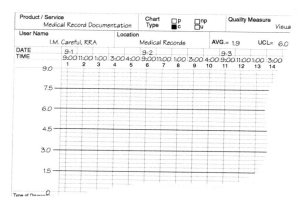

6. DRAW THE CENTERLINE AND CONTROL LIMITS.

Draw a dark horizontal line to represent $\bar{c}$. Draw dark dashed lines to represent the upper and lower control limits on the chart. If the lower control limit is zero, the dark dashed line is optional. Label each line respectively (UCL$_c$, LCL$_c$, $\bar{c}$). The example completed through this step is shown below.

7. PLOT THE VALUES ON THE CHART.

Plot a point on the chart for each c value on the vertical line that corresponds to each subgroup. Connect the dots with straight lines. The example completed through this step is shown below.

ATTRIBUTES CONTROL CHART

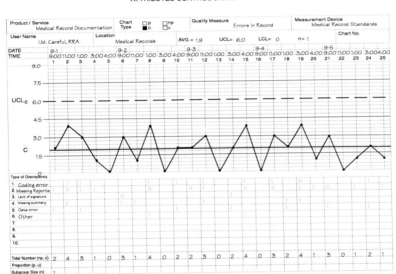

8. INTERPRET THE CONTROL CHART.

The c-chart is interpreted using the same basic rules for all control charts. Chart interpretation is explained further in the "Chart Interpretation" section. However, the basic rules for interpreting out-of-control conditions are listed below.

1. Any point lying outside the control limits.

2. Run of seven points:

   a. seven or more points in a row above or below the centerline
   b. seven or more points in a row going in one direction, up or down

3. Any nonrandom pattern, including the following typical cases:

   a. too close to the average
   b. too far from the average
   c. cycles

The example chart does not show any out-of-control situations. The variability present in the system is due to common causes and can be reduced only by changing the system in some way. In this case, the group found that most of the defects were due to missing diagnostic reports. Through further investigation, they discovered the majority of the reports were from Radiology. The group found the Radiology process for submitting final reports for inclusion in the medical records was performed very differently, depending upon who was working a shift. Identifying and standardizing a "best method" relieved this situation and the group was able to focus on its other key discrepancy areas.

When systems are declared to be stable, the control limits calculated previously are simply drawn onto new chart paper as subgroups continue to be collected. This will allow the clinical team or process owner to make decisions about the system's stability as each new subgroup is plotted. New control limits are calculated only when a change is made to the system.

 REMEMBER

1. A c-chart records the number of nonconformities per subgroup.

2. The characteristics being counted must be operationally defined before data collection begins.

3. The subgroup size must remain the same for all subgroups.

GETTING THE MOST FROM C-CHARTS

Getting the most from control charts means being able to use them for several different purposes as you make improvements.

When beginning to work on system improvement, **assess stability** of the system. The purpose of assessing stability is to analyze the factors which contribute to variability. Pick an important quality characteristic of the outcome and track it over time with a control chart. In health care, such a chart might be the number of errors in a medical record from a constant subgroup size of five. The use of a c-chart requires a constant sample size, but not necessarily a subgroup of one. A subgroup of 20 medical records, for example may be appropriate so long as it is always 20. Many factors influence the overall variability of a system, but until this first chart is made, one does not know whether to begin to work on common or special causes.

Once system stability is assessed, pay special attention to the need to **stratify data**. Sometimes you will find sources of variability this way. Inpatient medical records may contain more errors coming from Surgery than any other department. Or you may find that omission of provider signature is the nonconformity that occurs most often. You may find in a major teaching facility that entirely different results appear among specific providers, provider groups, ancillary departments, and so on. You must select your subgroups and record your data in a way that allows you to check for stratification by time, location, symptom, type, provider, etc. to better understand sources of variation.

To **generate improvement theories**, move your investigation upstream in the process to focus on the system elements that contribute to variability. They may be the causes identified on your cause and effect diagram. Often you need to apply control charts to the process or causal variables to tell whether they are themselves stable. Reduce the variability or number of nonconformities in each of these factors and you will reduce the overall system variability. Suppose you study Hospital A's method for completing medical records and discover that its definition of a completed medical record is different from the other 4 hospitals in your system. This method may account for the difference in completeness between that hospital and the other hospitals you observed.

Standardize the correct definition for completed medical record, replicate it in all hospitals, and continue to track the number of errors per five records. The control chart used in this way will help you decide if the standardized definition really makes a difference and whether the medical record documentation system has been improved.

The question of **when to calculate new control limits** often arises here. Should you calculate new limits when you have standardized and replicated the correct definition of a complete medical record? Yes! But wait until you see statistical evidence that the change has had an impact on your variable, such as a system shift or out-of-control condition. (Note: when recalculating control limits after a system change, use only those subgroups collected since the change occurred.) In general, once control limits are calculated, they are simply projected onto new forms as additional data is gathered so the operator has an ongoing way to assess stability as soon as a new subgroup is gathered and recorded. When you make a system change, you must write it on the chart. This way you can identify exactly which points on the chart correspond to the new method—and begin with those when you recalculate limits.

Finally, using the control chart for **standardization** means maintaining data collection throughout operation. Imagine that you had studied errors on medical records over six months, made changes to standardize and replicate methods, and immediately stopped taking data. What would happen? First, you would have only perception and opinion to tell you whether you had made improvements by your action. More importantly, you would have no way to identify unusual sources of variability that may crop up as hospitals continue to complete medical records in the standardized method now being used. Maybe the clinical records departments begin to identify parts of the medical record standards that no longer apply or some of the standards become obsolete or are changed by the regulator. Perhaps the clinical records departments have an influx of new personnel. Or maybe one or more of the hospitals in the system begins to use electronic records. Without a control chart, there is no way to know if the system changes. Special causes will appear and you can see them only when you have the statistical knowledge to recognize them.

Using the control chart for standardization suggests a system that is well defined, one whose variables are understood and whose most important procedures and elements are standardized. In other words, stable, predictable systems are more likely to result when standards of operation are in place and executed routinely. Clearly, it can be expected that standards and methods will change as improvements are discovered, but it becomes the responsibility of the system owner to communicate such changes to all concerned to maintain the steady streams of variability which are inevitable in even the most well-controlled systems.

In most organizations, data is highly available in attribute form. As you refine your study of variation and move upstream in processes, you may find you have a greater need for variables data. In fact, variables data is more useful because it can often point to sources of variation.

WHAT IS IT?

A u-chart is an attributes control chart which shows how a system measured by the number of nonconformities per unit produced will change over time. A nonconformity can be anything that is present on an item that should not be or anything that is not present that should be. Examples are the number of errors from one day's medical bills or medical records, or complications per one month's CABGs, or errors on one day's admissions forms. A u-chart can be used to show the count or number of nonconformities for subgroup sizes that may or may not change.

The purpose of the u-chart is to identify the two types of system variation present (special and common). By identifying which causes of variation are present in the system, the correct improvement action can be planned. Without the u-chart (or any control chart), those acting on the system would continually make the mistake of overcontrolling or undercontrolling the system.

We would use a u-chart to assess stability of the system. Only then would team members know which kind of improvement action to plan. Once the improvement action is implemented, we would continue collecting data and use the chart to monitor improvement, to see if the action worked.

 WHAT DOES IT LOOK LIKE?

An example of a u-chart with variable subgroup size is shown below. Only those u-charts with subgroups that vary in size by more than 25 percent from the average subgroup size will have adjusted control limits as in the example below.

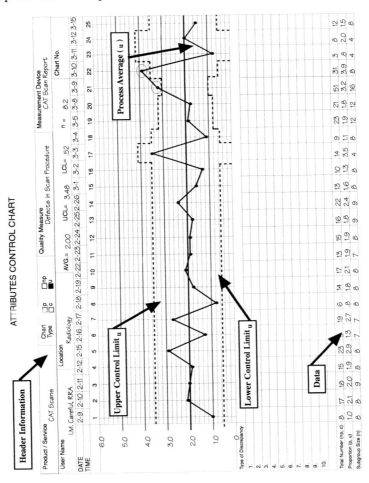

 # WHEN IS IT USED?

Note: A u-chart can handle a constant or variable subgroup size. However, if subgroups vary by more than 25 percent from the average subgroup size, special calculations are required. If the subgroup size is constant, a c-chart can also be used.

Use a u-chart when you can answer "yes" to all these questions:

1. **Do you need to assess system stability?** All control charts are used to assess stability of the system in order to minimize the chance of overcontrolling or undercontrolling the system.

2. **Does the data represent the number of nonconformities per subgroup?** Examples include number of defects or mistakes. Some examples are errors in a day's worth of medical bills or medical records, or defects in taking an x-ray (e.g., incorrect exposure, timing, patient position). If you wanted to classify the entire item (bill, record, x-ray) as defective (pass/fail) you would use p-or np-chart. Some examples are medical instruments (good or bad), invoices (correct or not), patient forms (complete or not), medical records (completed or not), x-rays (retaken or not).

3. **Have the possible nonconformities been operationally defined prior to data collection?** Operational definitions are especially important when collecting attributes data. The characteristics being charted should be operationally defined prior to collection. This is to insure that each data collector has the same idea of what the characteristic is and how to collect it so the results will be consistent. (See Operational Definitions.)

4. **Is the time order of the subgroups preserved?** Since the control chart is designed to make it easy to study system changes over time, the order of subgroups is critical. Mixing the order of subgroups would be like developing movie film with the frames mixed. It would be like treating the patient, then doing an initial assessment, then getting his history. This sequence is out of order.

HOW IS IT MADE?

These steps assume the header information is complete and the data has been previously collected and recorded on a data collection sheet or on control chart paper.

1. RECORD THE DATA.

Record the data in the data entry section on the chart paper. Fill in the row marked "Total Number" with the number of nonconformities (c) for each subgroup. Also fill in the row marked "Subgroup Size" with each subgroup size (n).

2. CALCULATE U FOR EACH SUBGROUP.

The number of nonconformities per unit is known as u. It is found by dividing the number (c) for each subgroup by the subgroup size (n).

$$u = \frac{number\ per\ subgroup}{number\ of\ units\ per\ subgroup}$$

$$= \frac{c}{n}$$

The u values should be recorded to one decimal place more than the c values.

3. CALCULATE THE AVERAGE NUMBER.

The average number is the average number per unit, $\bar{u}$. It is found by adding the "Total Number" row (c) and dividing by the sum of the "Subgroup Size" row (n).

$$\bar{u} = \frac{\sum c}{\sum n}$$

$$= \frac{c_1 + c_2 + c_3 + \ldots + c_k}{n_1 + n_2 + n_3 + \ldots + n_k}$$

$$= \frac{407}{204}$$

$$= 2.0$$

Record the value for $\bar{u}$ in the space marked "AVG" at the top of the chart.

Caution: Trying to calculate $\bar{u}$ by adding the subgroup u's and dividing by the number of subgroups is incorrect.

4. CALCULATE THE CONTROL LIMITS.

a. Calculate the average subgroup size.

The average subgroup size ($\bar{n}$) must be calculated in order to check whether any subgroups vary by more than 25 percent from $\bar{n}$. In addition, you need $\bar{n}$ for the control limit calculations. The average subgroup size ($\bar{n}$) is found by adding the "Subgroup Size" row and dividing by the number of subgroups taken (k).

$$\bar{n} = \frac{\sum n}{k}$$

$$= \frac{n_1 + n_2 + n_3 + \ldots + n_k}{k}$$

$$= \frac{204}{25}$$

$$= 8.2$$

b. Determine the subgroup size limits.

The easiest approach to variable subgroup size is to calculate the values for 25 percent above and below the average subgroup size ($\bar{n}$) before calculating control limits. Then each subgroup can be compared to these two numbers to determine where control limits must be calculated separately.

$$Upper\ subgroup\ size\ limit = \bar{n} \times 1.25$$

$$= 8.2 \times 1.25$$

$$= 10.25$$

$$Lower\ subgroup\ size\ limit = \bar{n} \times .75$$

$$= 8.2 \times .75$$

$$= 6.15$$

The control limits must be recalculated for each subgroup whose size falls outside the above two boundaries. In the example, six subgroups vary too much (subgroups 17, 19, 20, 21, 23, and 24).

c. **Calculate the control limits for all the data.**

First, the control limits are calculated using all the data on the chart—even if subgroups have been identified that must be calculated separately in Step 4b. The formulas for the control limits for the u-chart, UCL_c and LCL_c, are as follows:

$$UCL_u = \bar{u} + 3\sqrt{\frac{\bar{u}}{n}}$$

$$= 2.00 + 3\sqrt{\frac{2.00}{8.2}}$$

$$= 3.48$$

$$LCL_u = \bar{u} - 3\sqrt{\frac{\bar{u}}{n}}$$

$$= 2.00 - 3\sqrt{\frac{2.00}{8.2}}$$

$$= .52$$

The average subgroup size ($\bar{n}$) calculated in Step 4a is used for n in the formulas. Record the values calculated for the control limits in the spaces marked UCL and LCL at the top of the chart.

d. **Calculate the control limits for subgroups that vary excessively.**

If no subgroups were identified in Step 4b as varying by more than 25 percent from $\bar{n}$, control limit calculations are complete. If subgroups were identified, separate control limits must be calculated for each subgroup. The same formulas (above) will be used. However, instead of using $\bar{n}$ for n in the formula, use the individual subgroup size. For instance, in the example, the recalculated limits for subgroup 17 taken on March 3 are as follows:

$$UCL_{k=17} = 2.00 + 3\sqrt{\frac{2.00}{4}}$$

$$= 4.12$$

$$LCL_{k=17} = 2.00 - 3\sqrt{\frac{2.00}{4}}$$

$$= -.12$$

$$\approx 0$$

Since a negative nonconformity has no meaning, the lower control limit is rounded to 0.

5. DETERMINE THE SCALING FOR THE CHART.

The u-chart is scaled in the same manner as the c-chart. Remember that the increment value should be rounded (upward) so the dark reference lines can be labeled with easy-to-work with numbers such as multiples of 1, 2, 5, or 10. (See Step 5 in c-chart for details.)

6. DRAW THE CENTERLINE AND CONTROL LIMITS.

Draw a dark horizontal line on the chart to represent the average ($\bar{u}$). Draw dashed horizontal lines to represent each control limit. If separate control limits for any subgroups were calculated, remember to draw them in. Label the lines accordingly, UCL_u, LCL_u, $\bar{u}$.

7. PLOT THE VALUES ON THE CHART.

Plot a point on the chart for each u value for each subgroup. Connect the dots with straight lines.

8. INTERPRET THE CHART.

The u-chart is interpreted using the same rules as the c-chart and all other control charts. The basic rules for interpreting out-of-control conditions are listed below.

1. Any point lying outside the control limits.

2. Run of seven points:

    a. seven or more points in a row above or below the centerline
    b. seven or more points in a row going in one direction, up or down

3. Any nonrandom pattern, including the following typical cases:

    a. too close to the average
    b. too far from the average
    c. cycles

The example u-chart shows the system to be unstable. Two points, subgroups 21 and 22, lie outside the upper control limit. This indicates the presence of special causes of variation. The points should be investigated to determine the special causes of variation. Once discovered, the special causes should be permanently eliminated. In this case, the clinical team noted that the equipment was recalibrated just prior to subgroup 21. The technicians adjusted rapidly to bring the system back into control.

When systems are declared to be stable, the control limits calculated previously are simply drawn onto new chart paper as subgroups continue to be collected. This will allow the operator to make decisions about the system's stability as each new subgroup is plotted. New control limits are calculated only when a change is made to the system.

 ## OTHER HEALTH CARE EXAMPLES:

- The number of errors/discrepancies per one day's lines of transcription completed

- The number of errors/discrepancies per one week's mammograms shot

- The number of errors/discrepancies per number of procedures set up per day

- The number of errors/discrepancies per number of blood draws per week

- The number of complaints about inpatient meals per number of meals served per week

- The number of customer complaints per number of inpatient visits per week

CAUSE-AND-EFFECT DIAGRAM

CAUSE-AND-EFFECT DIAGRAM

 WHAT IS IT?

A cause-and-effect diagram (C & E diagram) is a picture of various system elements that may contribute to a problem or outcome. The C & E diagram was developed in 1943 by Professor Kaoru Ishikawa, President of the Musashi Institute of Technology in Tokyo. It is sometimes called an Ishikawa diagram or a fishbone diagram because of its resemblance to the skeleton of a fish.

The C & E diagram is used to identify possible variables influencing a problem, outcome, or effect. The graphic nature of the diagram allows groups to organize large amounts of information about a problem and pinpoint possible causes. It also encourages investigation of causes at many levels, improving odds that root or basic causes will be identified.

The C & E diagram is useful in both manufacturing and service or administrative settings. In health care it can be used to identify the variables influencing carpal tunnel syndrome outcomes or high risk pregnancy outcomes. The C & E diagram is also equally useful in identifying variables influencing the outcome of effect of support processes such as medication delivery, billing, purchasing, or scheduling. It can also be used to identify variables involved in general problems such as absenteeism, turnover, or waiting time.

The C & E diagram is used to find special or common causes of variation and to analyze causes. It can be used to solve unexpected or everyday problems of the system. Although the C & E diagram looks simple to make, it is not easy to do well. Kume, a Japanese quality professional, has said, "It may safely be said that those who succeed in problem solving in quality control are those who succeed in making a useful cause-and-effect diagram."[1]

---

[1] Hitoshi Kume, *Statistical Methods for Quality Improvement* (Tokyo, Japan: The Association for Overseas Technical Scholarship, 1988), p. 27.

52

WHAT DOES IT LOOK LIKE?

A completed example of a C & E diagram is shown below. A team in a hospital
made this C & E diagram to find possible causes for medications being delivered
late.

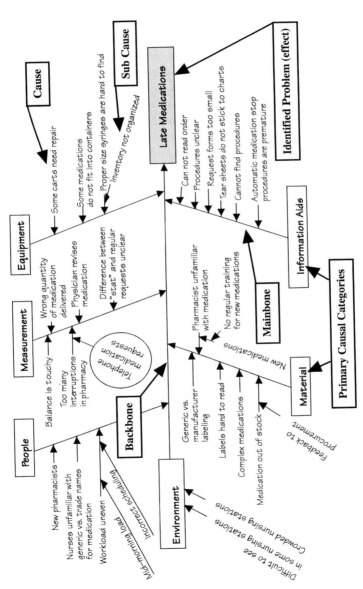

WHEN IS IT USED?

Use a C & E diagram when you can answer "yes" to one or both of these questions:

1. **Do root causes of a problem need to be identified?**

2. **Are there ideas and/or opinions about the causes of a problem?** Often people closely connected to the problem under study have formed opinions about what causes the problem. These opinions may conflict or may fail to express the root causes. Using a C & E diagram makes it possible to collect all these ideas for study from several points of view.

 # HOW IS IT MADE?

1. IDENTIFY THE PROBLEM.

The problem (effect) is usually in the form of a quality characteristic, which a group wants to improve or control. The problem should be specific and concrete: late medications, long ER waits, poor carpel tunnel outcomes, vascular complications, Coronary, Artery Bypass Graft, etc. "Late medications" is the identified problem in the example.

2. RECORD THE PROBLEM STATEMENT.

Write the identified problem on the far right side of the paper and allow space for the remainder of the diagram to the left. It is a good idea to use a very large space such as a chalkboard, easel and pad, or dry-erase board to construct the diagram. Draw a box around the problem statement.

3. DRAW AND LABEL THE MAIN BONES.

Draw and label the main bones of the diagram's skeleton. The main bones represent the primary input/resource categories or causal factors. The traditional labels for these areas are materials, methods, machine, people, and environment. Usually, the first four (materials, methods, machine, and people) are listed on the big bones (two on each side of the backbone) and the last area, environment, listed on the end of the backbone or tail. Draw a box around each heading. Shown below is an example of the traditional C & E diagram skeleton.

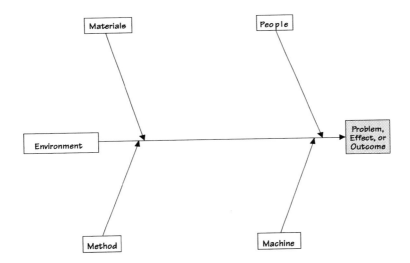

The main bones can be labeled with any general cause category that fits the particular problem. After you become more familiar with constructing the diagram, you may want to customize the diagram to each problem or to your organization. The example completed through this step is shown below. Notice that the primary groups are stated slightly different from the traditional five listed on the previous page.

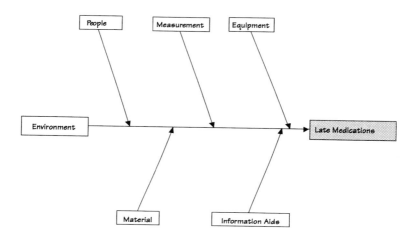

4. BRAINSTORM FOR PROBLEM CAUSES.

Brainstorm for causes to the problem. This is the most important step in constructing the C & E diagram. Ideas generated in this step will drive the selection of root causes. It is important that only causes of the problem, not symptoms or solutions, are identified. Listings such as "need new equipment" imply solutions. Avoid this terminology. Solutions are generated only after the root cause has been identified. Read the text on the following page to learn more about brainstorming.

Brainstorming is the free, uninhibited generation of ideas, usually in a group setting.

GOALS

1. **To generate a wide variety and extensive number of ideas.** This goal is based on the principle that brainstorming is synergistic—that is, it produces a greater total effect than that which can be produced by individual effort.

2. **To insure that everyone in the group becomes involved in the problem-solving process.** All ideas generated are potentially valid and each participant should feel that he or she can contribute.

3. **To insure that nothing is overlooked.** If ground rules are followed, individuals engaged in brainstorming will have confidence that every possible idea has been introduced and considered.

4. **To create an atmosphere of creativity and openness.** Properly run, a brainstorming session can unleash otherwise constrained minds to areas of creativity.

RULES

So that these goals can be reached, the group should follow the rules listed below when participating in a brainstorming session.

1. **No criticism allowed.** No evaluation or criticism of others' ideas during the process should occur. Criticism will only inhibit participants from being open about their ideas.

2. **Each person has equal opportunity to express ideas.** No one person may dominate idea offering. This can be accomplished by going around the table in an orderly fashion, giving each person a turn.

3. **Quantity over quality.** As many ideas as possible should be generated. Ideas breed other ideas.

4. **Piggybacking or hitchhiking is encouraged.** These terms mean that participants try to get ideas from the ideas of others. Frequently one participant's idea will trigger another, slightly different idea.

HOW TO RUN A BRAINSTORMING SESSION

1. **Select a recorder and group facilitator.** This person records the ideas as they are generated and makes sure the group does not violate any ground rules.

2. **Generate ideas.** Begin idea generation by going around the group in an orderly fashion allowing one idea per person. A participant with more than one idea should write them down to be given in turn. If participants do not have ideas when it is their turn, they can pass.

3. **Record the ideas.** As the ideas are generated, the recorder records them on flip chart paper. It is important that the ideas are displayed so the group can see them. As easel chart pages are filled, they should be taped to the wall. Seven to ten minutes is the recommended time for a brainstorming session.

Record the causes on the diagram. Each cause is recorded on a line or bone attached to the area under which it falls. Causes should be generated on varying levels. More levels can be generated by asking "why" to causes. The more levels that are generated, the better. The root cause to the problem may be located several levels deep. For instance, under the category "people" on the example, three causes were identified: new pharmacist, workload uneven, and nurses unfamiliar with generic versus trade names for medications. The group asked, "Why is the workload uneven?" The answers were mid-morning load and incorrect scheduling. Subcauses are placed on lines (small bones) under the cause to which they apply.

You may not have additional levels for every identified cause. What appears on the diagram is what was generated by the group during brainstorming. The example completed through this step is shown below.

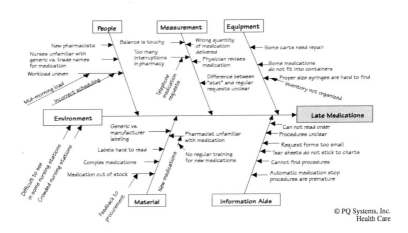

5. IDENTIFY THE MOST LIKELY CAUSE CANDIDATES.

At this stage, the group is choosing only cause candidates. The causes identified are only educated guesses and must be verified with more data. Identify these candidates through extensive discussion. Not all of the causes in the diagram are necessarily closely related to the problem; the group should narrow its analysis to the most likely causes. It may even be helpful to make a new diagram deleting unlikely causes. The most likely cause(s) chosen by the group should be identified as a candidate(s) by circling it or marking it with an asterisk.

In the example, the group identified "telephoned medication requests" as the most likely cause of late medications. The group in this case verified the cause by collecting data to make a scatter diagram. (See "Scatter Diagram.") The scatter diagram showed a correlation between the number of telephoned medication requests and the number of late medications. The group now has data that supports its educated guess. The completed C & E diagram is shown below.

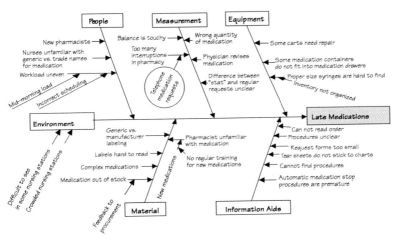

REMEMBER

1. The C & E diagram is a graphic way to display a lot of cause information in a compact space.

2. The C & E diagram helps people move from opinions to theories that can be tested.

3. The C & E diagram appears simple but is critical to understanding how to improve systems and may be difficult to make.

GETTING THE MOST FROM C & E DIAGRAMS

Once cause candidates have been chosen from the C & E diagram, new data must be gathered to verify causes. Verify causes in two ways: first, verify that causes produce the effect they seem to produce; and second, verify that in the absence of these causes the effect is not produced. In other words, test that the effect is produced when the cause is there, and not produced when the cause is not there. It is difficult to prove the exact strength of the relationship between a cause and an effect. Many different factors can produce one effect. To achieve the greatest improvement, identify, verify, and remove the cause that contributes most to producing the effect.

Cause-and-effect analysis can be carried out at multiple levels. First, do a primary analysis to identify the most likely cause. Next, this most likely cause becomes the effect (or problem statement) for a second C & E diagram. Using the C & E diagram in this way helps focus the analysis to get to the root cause of the problem. (See the diagrams below for an illustration.)

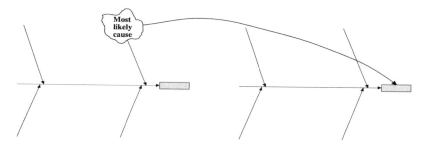

Diagram 1: First Level

Diagram 2: Second Level

Cause-and-effect diagrams can also be used for purposes other than root cause analysis. The format of the tool lends itself to planning, for instance. For example, a group could brainstorm the "causes" of a successful patient education program, a new employee information newsletter, or an ideal laboratory data storage and retrieval system.

OTHER HEALTH CARE EXAMPLES

- Delays in ER

- Long clinic wait times

- Excessive waits for radiology appointments

- OR delays

- Inability to get through on phone lines

- Excessive cost in a particular process or service

- Errors in billing, records, admitting, documentation, etc.

- Complications related to a particular surgery or treatment

- Unplanned readmissions

- Fluid overload or another adverse patient condition in inpatients

- Nosocomial infections among ventilator patients

- Causes of patient falls or needlesticks

- Billing delays

CHART INTERPRETATION

CHART INTERPRETATION

 ## WHAT IS IT?

Control chart interpretation is the process of analyzing the chart to understand the performance of the system being studied. Chart interpretation is a matter of asking key questions and recognizing patterns. With only minor differences, the same approach works for all kinds of control charts.

The purpose of all control charts is to help people who are managing systems to make the right decisions about how to control or run them. We have already mentioned the two kinds of mistakes that can be made: mistakes of undercontrol and mistakes of overcontrol. To understand these mistakes better, think of riding with a new driver. Every lane change is traumatic; every car turning ahead is cause to hit the brakes. In fact, ordinary driving events seem unusual to the new driver, so he or she is likely to overcontrol. The result: a jerky ride at best, a dangerous one at worst. On the other extreme, the new driver takes the car out in a rainstorm, drives at the speed limit, applies his brakes as usual for a stop sign, and skids helplessly into the intersection. He fails to recognize unusual conditions, acts normally, and undercontrols. Control charts do for system managers what learning does for the new driver—they help to tell the difference between ordinary and unusual events so the best course of action can be taken. Working on the causes of ordinary events is called working on "common causes" of variability; working on the causes of unusual events is called working on "special causes" of variability.

System improvement will not come magically by making a control chart. System improvement comes only from planned change of the right kind. Control chart users must interpret the control charts they have made to assess stability so they know what kind of action to take—action on ordinary events or action on unusual events. After they have made a planned change, they continue to interpret the control chart to tell if they have been successful when trying out their improvement theory. Interpretation is most effective when done in real time. Real time means that the chart is interpreted as the points are being plotted.

The same signals that can point to the right kind of action for improvement can also help to sort out problems of stratification. In this case, control charts are used to compare data separated by time, location, symptom, or type. A team might stratify a month's worth of unplanned readmissions by DRG, for example, to test for possible differences that could lead to a theory for improvement.

⌒○○ WHAT DOES IT LOOK LIKE?

Control chart interpretation is a mental process, not an object like the control chart. It is not possible to show a picture of it. What we can do, though, is to picture the process with a flow chart. The flow chart shows that control chart interpretation is a series of questions leading to a decision about the stability of the system.

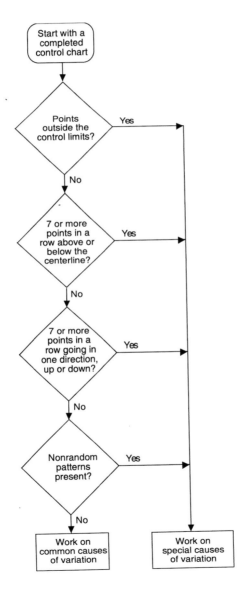

WHEN IS IT USED?

Because every control chart is made to be the basis for action, there is never a question about when to use chart interpretation. Interpret every control chart, and reinterpret it with the addition of every new point.

 HOW TO INTERPRET CONTROL CHARTS

Note: Since the questions for interpretation are similar for all types of control charts, illustrations here will be a variety of both types of charts, attributes and variables.

1. LOOK FOR ANY OF THE FOLLOWING UNSTABLE CONDITIONS:

   a. Any point lying outside the control limits;

   b. Run of seven points:

      i. seven or more points in a row above or below the centerline
      ii. seven or more points in a row going in one direction, up or down;

   c. Any nonrandom pattern, including the following typical cases:

      i. too close to the average
      ii. too far from the average
      iii. cycles.

Each of these conditions will be explained in more detail with the help of examples.

a. Any point lying outside the control limits

This is the quickest and easiest test for system stability. Look above the upper control limit and below the lower control limit to see whether any points fall in those regions of the chart. Circle any points found there. (When there are two charts together as with $\overline{X}$-R, $\widetilde{X}$-R, $\overline{X}$-s, and X-MR, look at both charts.) This is probably the result of a special cause which was corrected, either intentionally or unintentionally, very quickly. The $\overline{\overline{X}}$-R chart below shows points outside the control limits.

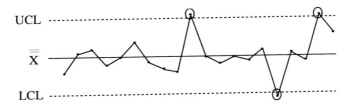

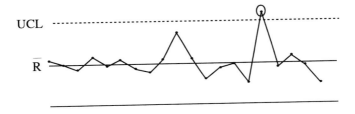

b. Run of seven points

i) Seven or more points in a row above or below the centerline

To apply this test, look for groups of points above or below the average or centerline. Count consecutive points. Circle any groups of seven or more. Multiple groups may appear, and all such groups should be circled. This is probably the result of a shift in one of the system resources (materials, people, methods, environment, information aids, equipment, and measurement). The following p-chart shows two groups—one with seven above the centerline and one with nine below.

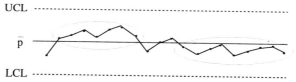

ii) Seven or more points in a row going in one direction, up or down

For this test, look for groups of points moving upward or downward in succession. Count consecutive points, including horizontal runs within the run. Circle any groups of seven or more. If multiple groups appear, circle them all. This is probably the result of a trend in one of the system resources. The $\widetilde{X}$-R chart below shows a group of eight medians moving downward.

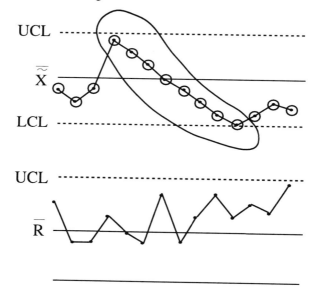

c. Any nonrandom patterns

This is the most complex of the tests for stability. If the system were in control or stable, you could expect to be able to imagine tilting the chart on end and letting all the points slip down to form a normal distribution or bell-shaped curve (see following sketch). Therefore, about half of the points will fall above and half below the average. If we divide the distance between the centerline and the control limits into three equal divisions upward and three more downward, we expect to find about two thirds of the total plot points in the middle two regions. We would not expect to find any repeatable patterns in the data.

Patterns in the data are not random, and are, therefore, cause for investigation. To apply this test, look for the following patterns in the chart: too close to the average, too far from the average, and cycles.

i) Too close to the average

Notice that nearly all the points lie close to the average. This pattern may indicate:

1. Edited data (attributes).

2. Reduced variability without recalculation of control limits (variables).

3. Small sample size (attributes). Using a p- or np-chart, a sample size less than 50 frequently yields this pattern.

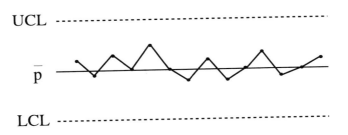

ii) **Too far from the average**

Notice how most of the points in both the average and range charts that follow are close to one control limit or the other. This pattern may indicate that subgroups have been drawn from two sources and the data has been mixed. If so, stratify (separate) the data and replot on two charts. Or it may indicate that overcontrolling or tampering is occurring. The third likely reason for this pattern is a large sample size with an attributes chart. Sample sizes larger than 200 for a p- or np-chart frequently yield this pattern.

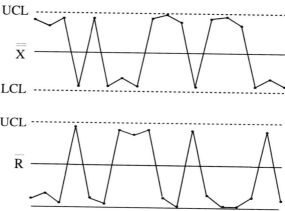

iii) **Cycles**

The data rises and falls in a rhythmic pattern—definitely not in a random pattern. This could be caused by some regular, periodic change in the system.

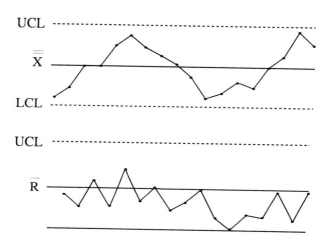

2. DECLARE THE SYSTEM IN CONTROL (STABLE) OR OUT OF CONTROL (UNSTABLE).

Only if the chart passes all the tests above can the system be said to be in control or stable. The chart below reflects a stable system. Teams will often find that their first control charts show out-of-control conditions.

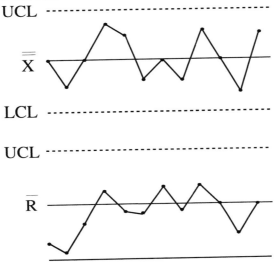

3. RESPOND TO THE INFORMATION ON THE CHART.

If the system is in control, the team can go straight to work on the causes of ordinary events or common causes. The members may need to reduce variability in the inputs to the process; they may need to study the entire set of causes that affect their data before they see what improvements to try. A team working on the system of incoming appointment phone calls to the clinics has found the total number of daily calls to be in control. They could not understand why complaints from customers about busy signals at the switchboard were on the rise. Finding the cause of trouble would take more study. Only when they separated the data by hour of day did they uncover the source of trouble.

If the system is out of control, the chart user should investigate all out-of-control conditions to discover what unusual or special causes were present to affect the system. When investigating special causes, first check for math error in the plotting or calculating of the out-of-control points. If no math error is found, go back to the information recorded on the control chart—date, time, people, equipment, materials, or methods changes—to find likely causes. Causes that lead to trouble should be prevented from recurring. The chart below shows an unusually high number of unplanned readmissions from patients who were discharged during four days of the previous month. The chart user noticed that all those points outside the limits occurred on Fridays. The next step is to see why Friday's discharges are different from any other day's. Once the special difference is found, perhaps it can be prevented.

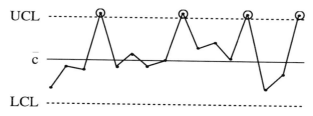

Not all out-of-control conditions indicate trouble. The X-MR chart below, of days between repeat Caesarean Sections shows the system be unstable because seven points in a row are above the average. But in this case, this pattern is good because it means the hospital is experiencing longer periods of time between repeat C-Sections (physicians are performing fewer repeat C-Sections). Finding out what has led to the improvement and making sure that the special cause stays in the system may be keys to continued improvement.

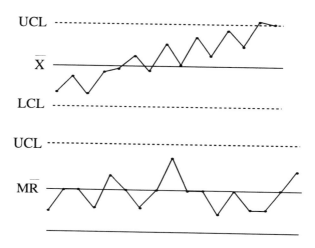

 REMEMBER

1. All control charts should be interpreted after their control limits are calculated.

2. Control charts give statistical signals that guide those involved in system improvement: Interpretation is a matter of reading those signals. Interpretation is most effective when it is done in real time by people closest to the process.

3. Interpretation is a mental process based on questions and pattern recognition.

4. Not all out-of-control signals mean trouble.

5. The basic rule for interpretation is to look for unstable conditions:

    a. Any point lying outside the control limits;

    b. Run of seven points:

        i. seven or more points in a row above or below the centerline
        ii. seven or more points in a row going in one direction, up or down;

    c. A nonrandom pattern, including the following typical cases:

        i. too close to the average
        ii. too far from the average
        iii. cycles.

 GETTING THE MOST FROM CONTROL CHART INTERPRETATION

Two additional topics will be discussed here: specific interpretation issues for various control charts, and advanced rules for analysis of control chart patterns.

CHART-SPECIFIC INTERPRETATION ISSUES

1. **For Variables Charts**

    a. Consider together the two messages that variables charts send about each subgroup: the central location and the variability. Look at the variability measure (range or standard deviation) to tell how different data points within the subgroup are from each other. Look at the central location (average or median) to tell where the middle of the subgroup is. The points on the chart, taken in pairs, are the basic statistics describing the subgroups.

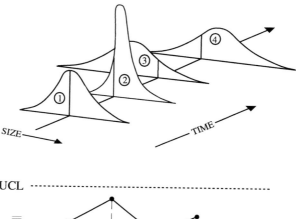

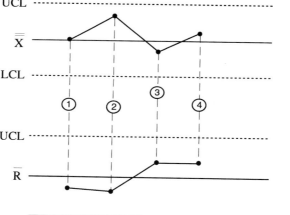

b.   Interpret the chart for variability first—whether the range, the moving range, or the standard deviation. If out-of-control conditions exist here, address them before going on. Too much variability in the subgroups can be a very difficult challenge, but until this variability is reduced, it does little good to work on the target or central location. Think about the marksman's problem to understand this idea. If the pattern of shot varies widely, one time tight and another time loose, all the marksman can do is aim at the middle of the target and hope for the best (see Figure A). If he can tighten up the shot pattern, though, he can place shots to his choosing inside the target (see Figure B).

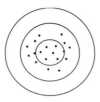

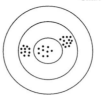

Figure A   Figure B

c. Keep in mind that the points plotted on an X-MR chart are actual
    readings from the system, not averages or medians. This is the only
    control chart where patient or payer targets or requirements can be
    compared directly to control limits. Also, remember that the
    individual readings may not be normally distributed for a stable
    system. They may be skewed because the system is naturally
    bounded on one side. Characteristics such as timeliness are bounded
    by zero.

2. For Attributes Charts

a. Always note which direction of movement for the points reflects
    improvement. A p-chart on proportion of post organ transplant
    rejections would reflect improvement by data moving downward to
    smaller percents. A p-chart for the proportion of patients undergoing
    knee replacement who report return to full functioning (return to
    work and social activities) post surgically would reflect
    improvements by points moving upward. It is a good idea to indicate
    the direction of improvement on the chart, as shown in the two
    examples below.

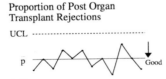

Proportion of Post Organ
Transplant Rejections

Proportion of Post Knee Replacement
Patients Regaining Full Function

b. Even though the p-chart and u-chart with variable limits look strange,
    interpret them in the usual way. Consider each point only as it
    compares to its own limits. Variable limits make some points "in"
    that would be "out" compared to limits for other samples, and vice
    versa. Take point F on the chart on the next page, for instance.
    Compared to the limits for point E it would be "out," but compared
    to its own limits it is "in." This chart reflects performance of a stable
    system.

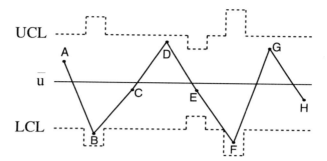

ADVANCED INTERPRETATION RULES

Use these advanced rules sparingly. There is a tendency to overcontrol the system when using these rules. Use them as a resource only when there is some doubt concerning system stability.

1. **Trends**

   Notice that the plot of averages drifts upward on this example even though there is no group of seven points in a row. This pattern indicates a gradual change in the measured characteristic over time.

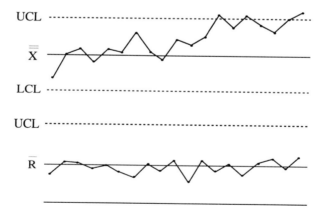

2. Clusters

Data appears in groups even though there is no group of seven points in a row. This pattern suggests that the system is "jumping" from target to target.

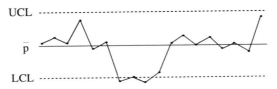

3. Sawtooth

Observe how the range points alternate above and below the centerline in this example. For some reason, alternate subgroups have greater and smaller ranges.

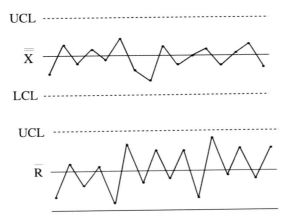

4. Two Out of Three Points Beyond the 2-Sigma Limits

The control limits that are drawn on control charts are located 3 standard deviations away from the average (or centerline) of the chart. We call these 3-sigma control limits. (Recall that sigma is the name of the symbol that stands for standard deviation.) The distance from the centerline to the control limits can be divided into three equal parts, 1 sigma each. If two out of three consecutive points on the same side of the average lie beyond the 2-sigma limits, the system is unstable. The X̄-R chart below demonstrates this rule.

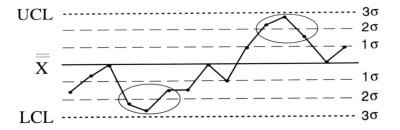

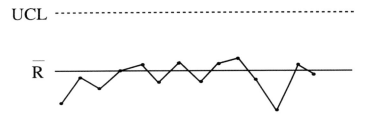

5. **Four Out of Five Points Beyond the 1-Sigma Limits**

When four out of five consecutive points lie beyond the 1-sigma limits on one side of the average, the system is declared unstable. The X-MR chart below demonstrates this rule.

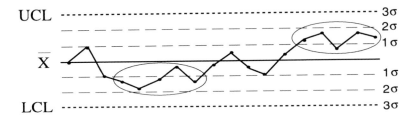

The ultimate goal of using control charts is to make improvements to the system. Whether a system is found to be stable or unstable is neither good nor bad. Either condition provides knowledge about the system and an opportunity for improvement. Although eliminating special causes of variation to bring a system under control is a step forward, don't stop there. Work on common causes of variation through planned change (P-D-S-A) cycle) to improve the system.

CHECK SHEET

CHECK SHEET

 WHAT IS IT?

A check sheet is a tool for collecting data in a consistent form. Check sheets provide an easy, structured way of recording data as it is collected. Also, they assure that each person collecting data will record it in the same way.

An effective check sheet depends on good design. To design a good check sheet, it is important to know how the data will be used, what you want to learn from the data, who will gather the data, where it will be gathered, and when it will be gathered. An unlimited number of formats for check sheet design can be used. The design is based on the data and on personal preferences. Organizations often develop their own formats for various types of check sheets.

The most common check sheets are arranged in columns or in matrices. The categories are generally listed along the left side with space to the right to make tally marks. Other information such as time or date can be listed across the top. This classic format can be used for both attributes and variables data. Once the check sheet is designed, it may be used to collect data on a single element at a given time or to compile the data from many check sheets. It is sometimes useful to compile all the collected data on one check sheet to make analysis or further use easier.

Check sheets are often used by groups to gather data. The collected data can be analyzed with other tools such as control charts, Pareto diagrams, and histograms. Most attributes control chart paper has a built-in check sheet at the bottom.

 WHAT DOES IT LOOK LIKE?

A completed check sheet is shown below. A home health care improvement team made this check sheet to collect the types of nosocomial infections occurring within their system (some 275 units).

Home Health Care Nosocomial Infections: Systems Wide

Data collected by: Mary T Walker, RN   Start: April 2

Location: Anytown, NM   Tel. 555-5555

Defect Types	Weeks											Total
	1	2	3	4	5	6	7	8	9	10	11	
UTI	I		I	I	I	I	I	I	I	I	I	10
URI		I	II		II	II		III	I	II	I	14
Wound	I		I	I			I			I	II	7
Communicable disease		I									II	3
TB	I								I			2
Conjunctivitis		I			I				I	I		4
Cullulitis	I	I	I	I		I	I		I	I		8
Hepatitis		I	I				I		II	I		6
Other infections	I		I				I			I		4
Total patients under care each week	76	70	81	64	72	65	72	81	83	91	76	

WHEN TO USE IT?

Use a check sheet when you can answer "yes" to all these questions:

1. **Is data to be collected?** Data must be collected before any improvements can be made. Data on the quality measure is collected first to establish a base from which to measure improvement; this is called baseline data. Data continues to be collected to monitor improvement and to ensure the improvement will hold.

2. **Is an organized format for collecting the data needed?** When collecting data, it is almost always best to use a standard form to minimize variation in recording the data. Also, a standard form makes it easier to use the data for the intended purpose.

3. **Will different people be collecting or using the data for the study or project?** Check sheets encourage consistency and provide guidance. A well-designed check sheet can cut down the time needed to train data collectors. A person needs only to follow the check sheet to record data correctly. For data users, a good check sheet minimizes disagreements and helps speed analysis.

 # HOW IS IT MADE?

These steps assume that a data-gathering plan has been formulated. In other words, it is known what data to gather, how to gather it, how much of it to gather, how often to gather it, where to gather it, and who will gather it.

1. LIST THE DATA NEEDS.

From the data-gathering plan, list all the data items that need to be included on the check sheet. Typical candidates in a health care setting are related to time, date, location, shift, provider, etc. This list of typical items is by no means complete. Specific projects will demand specific data.

Since the quality measure in the example is the number of Home Health Care Nosocomial Infections occurring within a specific Home Health System, the list of data needs will include all the possible type of key infections known. A good idea here is to also include an Other column. The list will also include information such as time period, date, numbers of infections found (sheet total figure) the data collector, the data collector's location and telephone number.

These are included as additional information so that data can be stratified or reorganized later, using a Pareto diagram or other analytical tool.

The list of data needs for the example is shown here.

Types of infections (defects): UTI
                                URI
                                Wound
                                Communicable disease
                                TB
                                Conjunctivitis
                                Cellulitis
                                Hepatitis
                                Other

Additional information: time period
                         date
                         total numbers of infections found
                         name of the person collecting the data
                         the data collector's location
                         the total number of patients under care that week
                         the data collector's telephone number

2. DECIDE ON CHECK SHEET FORMAT.

Discuss possible check sheet formats with members of the group or team. The check sheet format is based on the data to be collected. A format that provides the easiest way to record, read, and use the collected data should be chosen.

A check sheet for variables data is likely to be simply a lined sheet of paper to record the figures, with extra space for comments. The data entry area at the bottom of control chart paper often serves as the check sheet for variables data for control charts and histograms.

In the example, the check sheet was used to collect attributes data—number of infections by type noted within the observed home health system. After looking at data needs list made in Step One, the team decided on a columnar format. The types of infections (defects) will be listed on the left, with columns to the right indicating totals for each week to make tally (count) marks. There will be an area at the top of the sheet to enter the additional information such as date total numbers of infections found, name of the person collecting the data, the data collector's location, and the data collector's telephone number.

3. DESIGN AND PRODUCE THE CHECK SHEET.

Design or draw the actual check sheet form. Use space, lines, and other visual elements to create an easy-to-read and understandable form.

Produce the completed form by photocopying a clean drawing or using a computer or typewriter. The best form of reproduction available should be used to make the form clear and easy to read.

The check sheet design for the example follows.

Home Health Care Nosocomial Infections: Systems Wide														
Data collected by: Mary T Walker, RN						Start: April 2								
Location: Anytown, NM						Tel. 555-5555								
Defect Types	Weeks											Total		
	1	2	3	4	5	6	7	8	9	10	11			
UTI														
URI														
Wound														
Communicable disease														
TB														
Conjunctivitis														
Cullulitis														
Hepatitis														
Other infections														
Total patients under care each week														

4. REVIEW THE DESIGN.

The finished check sheet should be reviewed with the team and the data collectors who will be using it. The purpose of the check sheet, its format, and the method for gathering and recording data should be reviewed. The review is an open discussion about the strengths and weaknesses of the check sheet. Any changes suggested by the team or data gatherers should be made before the check sheet is used.

5. TEST THE CHECK SHEET.

The check sheet should be tested by beginning to gather data. After a short period of time, say one week, initial check sheets and data are analyzed to see if they meet the requirements of the data-gathering plan.

© PQ Systems, Inc.
Health Care

The check sheet should be revised if any problems are found in its use. Revisions must be made known to everyone using the form.

REMEMBER

1. A check sheet provides a format for collecting data.

2. A good check sheet design increases the efficiency of data use.

3. The check sheet is designed to make data gathering and analysis easier.

4. There are unlimited format designs for check sheets.

OTHER HEALTH CARE EXAMPLES

• Missed appointments per day in each clinic

• Reasons for late delivery of food carts to wards

• Sources of consults by clinic to a home health agency

• Open heart admission events to ICU

• Factors associated with LOS in excess of standards

FLOW CHART

FLOW CHART

WHAT IS IT?

A flow chart is a picture of any process (sequence of events, steps, activities, or tasks) that transforms inputs into outputs in a system. Flow charts are drawn with standard symbols that represent different types of activities or tasks.

There are many styles of flow charts, used for different kinds of processes, but only two styles will be shown here. The two are: deployment flow chart and process flow chart. Deployment flow charts are becoming increasingly recognized for their usefulness in improvement projects, and will be presented first.

Any style of flow chart can be drawn with various depths of detail. The style and depth chosen should be ones that give the most useful picture for the flow chart's intended purpose. One purpose of a flow chart is to define the system being studied, by describing and documenting the process. A flow chart can also be used to generate an improvement theory, by looking for ways to simplify, streamline, or redesign the process. In standardization, the flow chart can be used to describe and document the process, and to train people in its operation.

The value of drawing a flow chart is in describing the flow of materials (information, documents, people, or raw materials) as they are transformed into outputs. It is essential, however, that everyone can agree on and understand the process described by the flow chart. Therefore, it is important that everyone involved in designing, operating, or controlling the process helps to draw the flow chart.

⬯ WHAT DOES IT LOOK LIKE?

Shown below is an example of a flow chart created by a medical supply team trying to reduce variation in its purchasing operation process. This style of flow chart is called a "deployment"[1] flow chart, because it shows who is responsible, or deployed, to carry out each task or activity in the process.

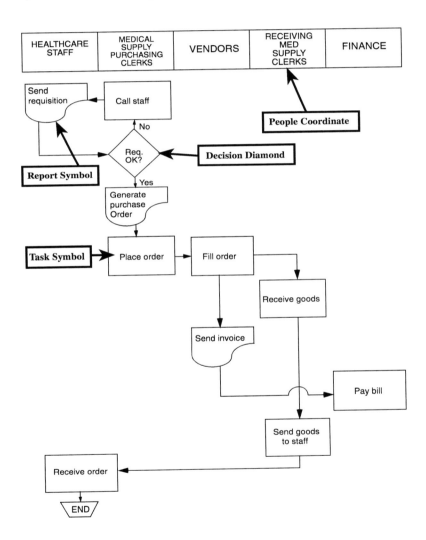

---

[1] Myron Tribus, "Deployment Flow Charting" (Los Angeles: Quality and Productivity, Inc., 1989).

 WHEN IS IT USED?

Use a deployment flow chart when you can answer "yes" to all these questions:

1. **Is a picture of a process needed?** Pictures are powerful communication tools. Because people can see the flow chart, they can more easily discuss how the process really works.

2. **Is it necessary to show the relationship of the people and the steps in a process?** Part of what makes processes difficult to describe is the overlap of departments or people. The deployment flow chart is especially designed to clarify who does what, when.

3. **Will the process be pictured as it actually operates?** Sometimes it takes persistence and discipline to see all the extra loops created when problems arise or things go wrong in the process. Yet the extra effort of drawing what really happens pays off when it is time to make improvements.

 HOW IS IT MADE?

1. DEFINE THE PROCESS BOUNDARIES.

Define the process boundaries by deciding where the picture of the process will start and stop. Within these boundaries (the starting and ending points) the group will focus its improvement efforts. It is important that participants agree on these boundaries before improvement studies are underway; everyone needs to know the exact focus for the project. Another way to accomplish this is to begin and end the flow chart with the customer.

In the example, the process being studied starts when the requisition is sent and ends when the goods are delivered to the appropriate health care staff members. The health care staff is the customer of this process.

2. OBSERVE THE PROCESS IN OPERATION.

Go to the process and walk through the sequence of steps from the starting point (identified in Step 1) to the ending point. Ask people how the work gets done. If possible, sketch the process and make notes on who does what in which order as you go.

3. DRAW A PEOPLE COORDINATE.

A people coordinate is a series of connected boxes drawn horizontally across the top of the chart indicating names of the people or departments involved in the process. Make one box for each person or department who is a key actor in the process. These key actors will probably be identified from the notes made when observing the process.

Write the names of the people or departments in the boxes from left to right, in the order in which they work on the materials flowing through the process. As you work on the flow chart, the sequence may need to be changed to make sure the picture is as clear as possible.

In the purchasing example, the people coordinate includes health care staff who need the medical supplies and services; medical supply purchasing clerks; receiving personnel, finance department personnel who do the work of paying for the medical supplies and services; and the vendors who supply the medical supplies and services. The people coordinate for the example is shown below.

HEALTHCARE STAFF	MEDICAL SUPPLY PURCHASING CLERKS	VENDORS	RECEIVING MED SUPPLY CLERKS	FINANCE

4. LIST MAJOR STEPS IN THE PROCESS.

On a separate sheet of paper, list the 5-10 major steps or activities in the process. This list can be generated from the notes taken while observing the process (Step 2). In the example the list is as follows:

send requisition
generate purchase order
place order
fill order
receive goods
send invoice
pay bill
send goods to staff
receive order

5. DRAW THE FLOW CHART, USING SYMBOLS.

Combine the information in Step 3 and Step 4 to draw the deployment flow chart. Draw the major steps in the process, identified in Step 4, using the symbols for deployment flow charting. The steps should be drawn from left to right in the order in which they are carried out. Each symbol, or step, should be placed below the correct person or department in the people coordinate. Connect the symbols with lines and arrows showing the direction in which the work, information, or materials flow. The symbols to use are those suggested by Dr. Myron Tribus, who has popularized the use of the deployment flow chart. The symbols and their meanings are shown below.

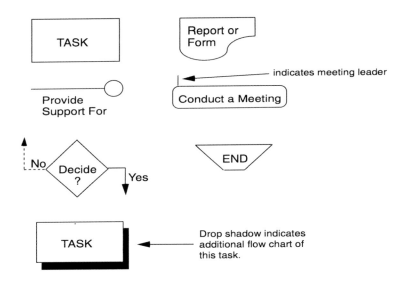

The medical supply purchasing team drew its flow chart this way:

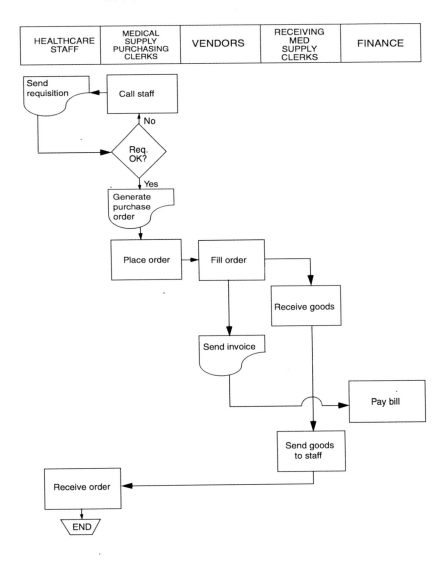

6. STUDY THE FLOW CHART.

Ways to study the flow chart depend on the purpose for which it was created. In an improvement project, the group may study the flow chart to determine where to gather data. The deployment flow chart is especially powerful for showing wasted time and effort due to complexity, redundancy, and non-value-added work such as rework and inspection. The following questions suggested by Dr. Tribus will help in looking for ways to improve the process.[2]

1. Look for horizontal lines. They define a supplier-and-customer relationship.

2. Ask if the supplier is trying to please the customer. If not, ask why.

3. Ask if the supplier and customer have agreed on what constitutes a "quality" job. Ask who defined quality. If it was not the customer, ask why not.

4. Look for the barriers which prevent the supplier from producing a quality output. Examine the budgetary process to see if false economies in the supplier's department are causing excessive expenditures in the customer's department.

5. Examine each decision process to see if the people who feed information to the decision maker understand the criteria which will be used in making the decision.

6. Inquire if the decision maker has told anyone about the criteria being used. Has the decision maker given any advice about the format in which the information should be presented?

7. Determine if statistics on the decision process are available. Do not depend on how people feel about the process; get hard data on how frequently the results are unsatisfactory. Use a Pareto diagram to determine the most frequent cause of an unsatisfactory decision.

---

[2] Myron Tribus, p. 22. "Deployment Flow Charting" (Los Angeles: Quality and Productivity, Inc., 1989).

 **REMEMBER**

1. A flow chart is a picture of a process (sequence of events, steps, activities, or tasks.)

2. Choosing the style and depth of detail for a flow chart depends on the purpose of the flow chart.

3. Everybody involved in the process should help make the flow chart and agree that it is an accurate picture of the process.

4. Flow charts are dynamic tools that should be changed when process changes are made.

 GETTING THE MOST FROM FLOW CHARTS

Getting the most from flow charts means using them on an ongoing basis and expanding them into more detail. Flow charts are drawn not only while doing an improvement project. They are also meant to be used as a tool for operating and controlling processes on a daily basis. Because they are a picture of the process or sequence of steps used to transform inputs into outputs, they should always represent the current, best known way to perform and control the process, and should be used by those who do the work as a job aid or set of instructions. As improvements are made in the process, new best known ways to operate and control the process should be documented in a new flow chart. When new employees are brought on the job, they should be trained to do the work using the flow chart as one of the training aids. Flowcharts can take the place of policies and procedures and are useful operating instructions because they show a picture of the process, the sequence of occurrences, and who should be doing what, when, and where. When producing quality manuals for either internal use or for accreditation by regulatory agencies, flow charts can be extremely useful to show how your processes work.

A flow chart can be simple or complex, depending on the detail required to make it useful. To design a new process, a flow chart would be drawn to describe the simplest way to make the highest quality, lowest cost output. If the purpose is to describe the process as it actually works, much more detail may be required.

Because medical supply team members in the example wanted to reduce the time required to receive materials and services, they expanded the flow chart to show added steps in the process when work is not done correctly. They also added a drop shadow to the "place order" task to show that another flow chart had been drawn for that step. The expanded flow chart is shown below.

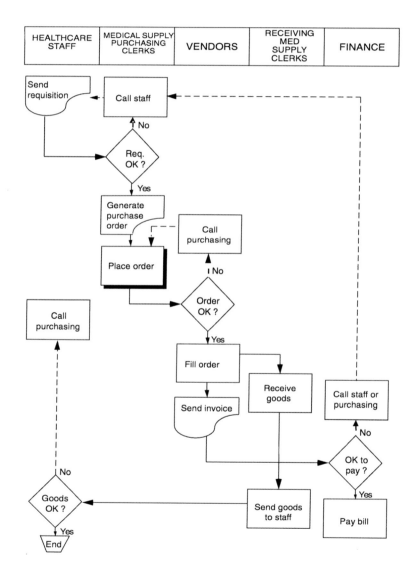

The drop shadow is one practical way to draw a flow chart with greater detail, while still making it easy to understand. The drop shadow allows one to "zoom" in on a task or activity in greater detail. The drop shadow is simply a darkened symbol immediately behind the symbol to be expanded or "zoomed." It means that another flow chart has been created for that symbol or step.

In the example, the medical supply purchasing team zoomed in on the "place order" activity for items over $1,000. The flow chart that this team created is pictured below.

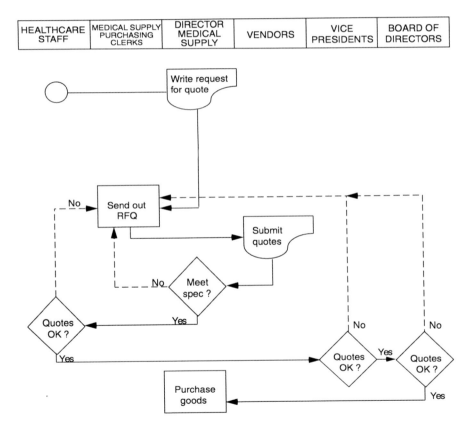

The process flow chart will be shown as one of the different kinds of flow charts that can be constructed.

WHAT IS IT?

The process flow chart is a picture of the major steps in a process. It is probably the simplest of all flow charts. Like other styles of flow charts, it is drawn using common symbols. The advantage to this simple flow chart is that it can be used in any situation or environment. In contrast to the deployment flow chart, it does not show the relationship of the people doing the work and the steps in the process.

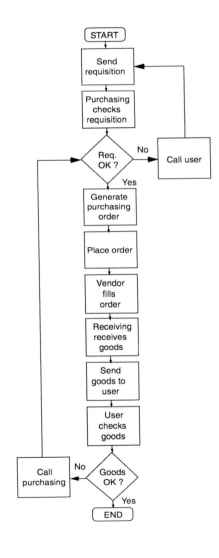 WHAT DOES IT LOOK LIKE?

Shown below is an example of a process flow chart using the data from the medical supply purchasing example in deployment flow charting. Notice that this flow chart communicates the same idea without the benefit of knowing the relationship between the steps and the key actors (the people coordinate).

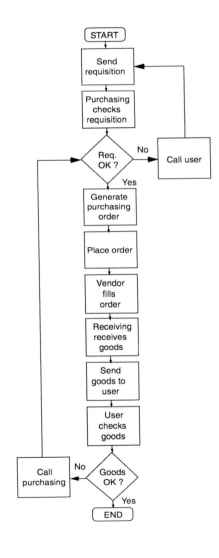

WHEN IS IT USED?

Use a process flow chart when you can answer "yes" to all these questions:

1. **Is a picture of a process needed?** Pictures are powerful communication tools. Because people can see the flow chart, they can more easily discuss how the process really works.

2. **Are actual steps in the process to be shown?** You want to show the process as it really operates rather than as it should operate.

3. **Is it unnecessary to show the relationship between the people doing the work and the work being done?** If the study focuses more on the tasks in the process rather than the people, you may want to do a process flow chart. A process flow chart also lends itself well to highly repeatable tasks.

 # HOW IS IT MADE?

1. OBSERVE THE PROCESS.

Go to the process and walk through the sequence of steps from beginning to end. Ask questions of people who are involved in the steps about how the work is done. If possible, sketch the process and make notes about each task in the process as you go.

2. LIST ALL STEPS IN THE PROCESS.

Make a list of all steps in the process. This list can be generated from the notes taken while observing the process. Consider writing all the steps on index cards or sticky notes so they can be arranged in sequence later on. Be sure to ask as many people as possible who are directly involved in the steps to help make the list.

3. ARRANGE THE STEPS IN SEQUENCE.

Next, the list of steps or cards should be arranged in the order in which they occur in the process.

4. DRAW THE FLOW CHART.

Use the common symbols shown below to draw the flow chart. Symbols representing each step should be drawn in a straight line, top to bottom, and connected by lines and arrows showing the direction of the flow of work, information, or materials in the process. The symbols used for the process flow chart are shown below.

5. STUDY THE FLOW CHART.

Study of the flow chart depends on the purpose for which it was made. In improvement projects, study usually means looking for opportunities to gather data, to eliminate unnecessary steps, to combine steps to improve the process, or to find better ways of operating the process.

OTHER HEALTH CARE EXAMPLES:

- Process of pediatric asthma treatment

- Process of diabetic assessment and education

- Process of Emergency Department triage

- Process of coronary artery bypass graft

- Patient assessment, treatment, and follow-up process

- Processes of admission, patient transportation, medication administration, patient scheduling, medical billing

- HMO enrollment process

HISTOGRAM

HISTOGRAM

🔍 WHAT IS IT?

A histogram is a bar graph representing the frequency of individual occurrences or classes of data. A histogram shows basic information about the data set, such as central location (mean, median, and mode), width of spread (range or standard deviation), and the shape.

The purpose of making a histogram is to gain knowledge about the system. This knowledge, gained from the basic information given by the histogram (central location, spread, and shape), will act as a guide to improve the system. From a stable system, predictions can be made about the future performance of the system. If the system were unstable, it would change from time to time and the histogram would have little predictive value.

The group uses a histogram to assess the system's current situation and to study results. The histogram's shape and statistical information help us know how to improve the system. After an improvement action is carried out, the group continues to collect data and make histograms to see if the theory has worked.

∽ᴏᴏ WHAT DOES IT LOOK LIKE?

A completed histogram is shown below. An outpatient clinic patient health educator constructed this histogram using data from the $\overline{X}$-R chart for the Adult Asthmatic Patient Respiratory Capability. The $\overline{X}$-R chart showed the system to be unstable. The patient and care provider successfully identified special cause in the last four subgroups (the patient was out of town and forgot to take medications). Deleting the four subgroups occurring due to special cause, the educator used the remaining 23 subgroups to make this histogram. (See Step 9 in $\overline{X}$-R for the stable control chart using the 23 subgroups.)

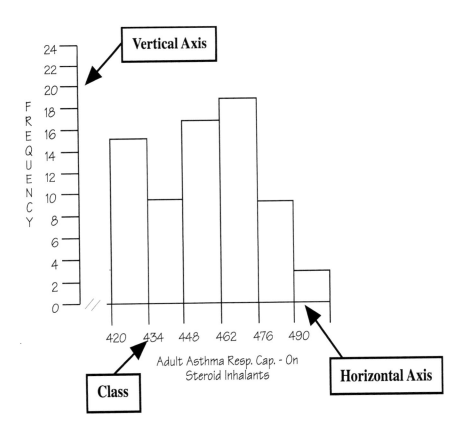

WHEN IS IT USED?

Use a histogram when you can answer "yes" to both these questions:

1. **Do you have a data set of related values, either attributes (counts) or variables data (measurement)?** For analyzing system performance, single readings or individual data points are of limited value. Much more can be learned from a group of data points because they reflect the system's variation. Using a histogram is one way to start learning from a group of data points.

2. **Is it important to visualize central location, shape, and spread of the data?** When it comes to data analysis, a picture is worth a thousand words. Seeing the form of the data makes it easier to understand the kind or pattern of variation the system is producing.

HOW IS IT MADE?

These steps assume that the data for the construction of the histogram has already been collected. The data can be collected especially to make a histogram or can come from the data entry section of a control chart. Once you have collected data for a control chart, that same data could be used to make a histogram. The data entry section of the control chart used for the example histogram is shown below.

VARIABLES CONTROL CHART

X – R CHART   Quality Measure   Chart No.

Product / Service	Asthma Care		Process	Respiratory Process			Specification Limits	N/A	
User Name	SKM		Location	Home		Measurement Device	Home Spirometer	Unit of Measure	MOSM

DATE	5-17	5-18	5-19	5-20	5-21	5-22	5-23	5-24	5-25	5-26	5-27	5-28	5-29	5-30	5-31	6-1	6-2	6-3	6-4	6-5	6-6	6-7	6-8
SAMPLE MEASUREMENT 1	430	460	450	475	440	480	420	480	450	430	470	475	480	500	450	465	460	445	430	450	500	420	420
2	420	480	470	470	450	450	460	480	470	450	445	480	450	450	430	470	470	450	.450	470	440	440	430
3	440	470	470	485	460	465	430	470	465	440	440	470	470	470	430	480	485	430	430	470	430	450	455
4																							
5																							
SUM	1290	1410	1390	1430	1350	1395	1310	1430	1385	1320	1355	1425	1400	1540	1310	1415	1415	1325	1310	1390	1370	1310	1305
AVERAGE, x̄	430	470	463.3	476.7	450.0	465.0	436.7	476.7	461.7	440.0	451.7	475.0	466.7	473.3	436.7	471.7	471.7	441.7	436.7	463.3	456.7	436.7	435.0
RANGE, R	20	20	20	15	20	30	40	10	20	20	30	10	30	50	20	15	25	20	20	20	70	30	35
NOTES																							

1. SELECT THE CLASSES.

a. Determine the number of classes.

To find the number of classes (or subdivisions) needed for the histogram, first count the number of data points in the data set. Then use the following table to choose the number of classes. As the table indicates, it is best to use no fewer than 5 classes (or subdivisions) or more than 20.

No. of Data Points	No. of Classes
Under 50	5 - 7
50 - 100	6 - 10
100 - 250	7 - 12
Over 250	10 - 20

There are 69 data points in the example, 23 subgroups of 3 observations each This table indicates between six and ten classes should be used for this many data points. Choose 6 for the example. The choice of the number of classes you want to use is only a rough estimate at this point. You can decide later to use more or fewer classes.

b. **Determine the class width and boundaries.**

The width of the class determines the range of data points in each class. Find the class width by dividing the range of the data set by the number of classes (found in Step a). The range is found by subtracting the smallest value in the data set from the largest.

$$Range = X_{highest} - X_{lowest}$$

In this example, the highest value in the data set is 500 and the lowest is 420. So the range is:

$$Range = 500 - 420$$

$$= 80$$

The class width for the example is:

$$Class\ Width = \frac{range\ of\ data\ set}{No.\ of\ classes}$$

$$= \frac{80}{6}$$

$$= 13.3$$

$$= 14$$

Round the class width to an easy number to work with. In the example, we rounded 13.33 to 14.

Next, select a starting number for the lower boundary of the first class. The lower boundary should be chosen so the lowest value in the data set is included in the first class. A convenient lower boundary for the example is 420, since the lowest value in the data set is 420.

To determine the lower boundaries for the remaining classes, begin with the lower boundary of the first class and add the class width. Continue adding class width until the number of classes is complete and all the data has been included.

The lower class boundaries for this example are:

$$420 + 14 = 434$$

$$434 + 14 = 448$$

$$448 + 14 = 462$$

$$462 + 14 = 476$$

$$476 + 14 = 490$$

$$490 + 14 = 504$$

In some cases, an extra class may need to be added so the highest data point will be included.

The upper boundary for each class is any number under or below the lower class boundary of the next class. For example, the upper class boundary for the first class is "under 434." This means that any number greater than or equal to 420 but less than 434 falls into the first class. This is done so that no point will fall on the boundary between two classes.

The classes for the example are:

420 to under 434

434 to under 448

448 to under 462

462 to under 476

476 to under 490

490 to under 504

2. RECORD THE DATA.

The easiest way to record the data is to create a check sheet listing the classes along the left side with space to the right to make tally marks. To record the data, make a tally mark beside the class in which each data point falls. Total the number of marks in each class. Shown below is the completed check sheet for the example.

CLASSES	TALLY	TOTAL
420 UNDER 434	ⅣⅠ ⅣⅠ ⅠⅠⅠ	13
434 UNDER 448	ⅣⅠ ⅠⅠⅠⅠ	9
448 UNDER 462	ⅣⅠ ⅣⅠ ⅣⅠ ⅠⅠ	17
462 UNDER 476	ⅣⅠ ⅣⅠ ⅣⅠ ⅠⅠⅠⅠ	19
476 UNDER 490	ⅣⅠ ⅠⅠⅠⅠ	9
490 UNDER 504	ⅠⅠ	2

3. PREPARE THE AXES.

a. Draw and label the horizontal and vertical axes.

Draw the horizontal and vertical axes to the desired length for the finished histogram. The two axes should be approximately the same length. Label each axis by writing the description of the measured data on the horizontal axis and the frequency of occurrence on the vertical axis. The example completed through this step is shown below.

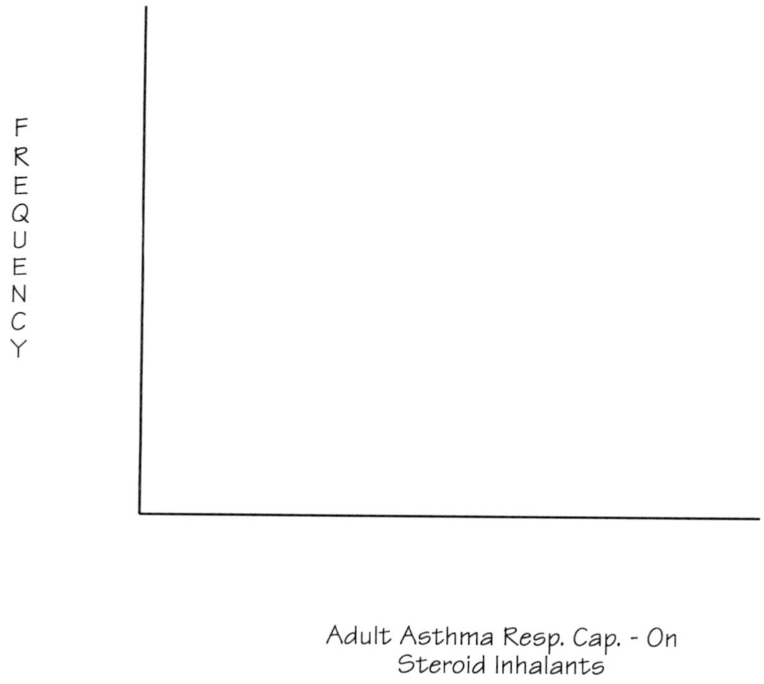

F
R
E
Q
U
E
N
C
Y

Adult Asthma Resp. Cap. - On
Steroid Inhalants

b. Scale and label each axis.

Divide the horizontal axis into the same number of equal divisions as the number of classes. The example has six classes, so the horizontal axis is divided into six equal divisions. Label each class at the lower boundary with its value.

The vertical axis should be divided into equal divisions to fit the frequency-of-occurrence range. The frequency-of-occurrence range can be found from the check sheet. On the check sheet for the example, the total frequency for the classes ranges from 2 to 19. The vertical axis should be scaled (divided) to accommodate these values. In the example, we divided the vertical axis into 20 equal parts, letting each part stand for 1. Label each increment starting at the origin with 0. The example completed through this step follows:

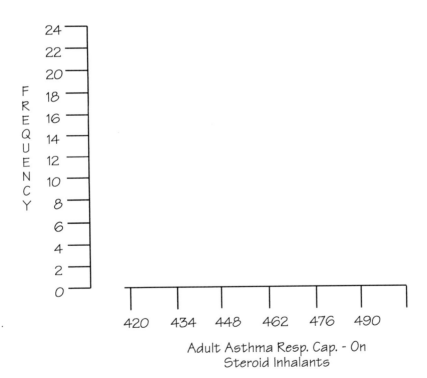

Adult Asthma Resp. Cap. - On
Steroid Inhalants

4. DRAW THE HISTOGRAM.

Draw a bar for each class with the height of each bar corresponding to the
frequency-of-occurrence shown on the check sheet (Step 2). The completed
example is shown below.

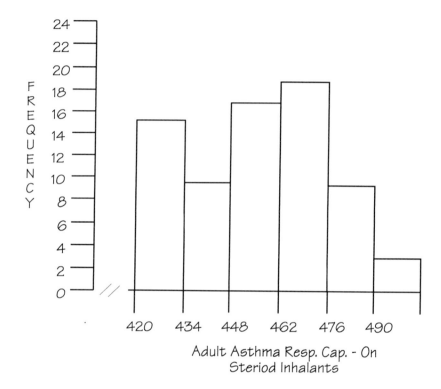

Adult Asthma Resp. Cap. - On
Steriod Inhalants

5. STUDY THE SHAPE.

Histograms form several common shapes. A somewhat bell-shaped picture (Figure 1 below) is usually a normal distribution. A bimodal shape (Figure 2) has two peaks. This shape may show that the data has come from two different systems. If this shape occurs, the two sources should be separated and analyzed separately.

The histogram can also form a skewed (tailing off) distribution to the right or left (Figures 3 & 4). A distribution skewed to the right is said to be positively skewed. This kind of distribution has a large number of occurrences in the lower classes and fewer in the upper classes. A distribution skewed to the left is said to be negatively skewed. This type of distribution has few occurrences in the lower classes and many in the upper classes. A skewed distribution can result when data is gathered from a system which has a boundary such as zero. In other words, all the collected data has values greater than zero.

Two other common distributions are the uniform and random distributions. The uniform distribution (Figure 5) provides little information. An example of a uniform distribution is the state lottery, in which each class has about the same number of elements. The random distribution (Figure 6) has no apparent pattern. Either of these patterns may describe a distribution which has several modes (peaks). Check to see if several sources of variation have been combined. If so, analyze them separately. If multiple sources of variation do not seem to be the cause of these patterns, different groupings can be tried to see if a more useful pattern results. This could be as simple as changing the starting and ending points of the classes, or the number of classes. Frequently, a uniform distribution just means that the number of classes is too small. Similarly, a random distribution may mean that there are too many classes.

Figure 1

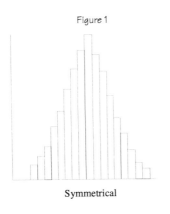

Symmetrical

Figure 2

Bimodal

Figure 3

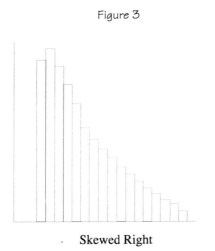

Skewed Right

Figure 4

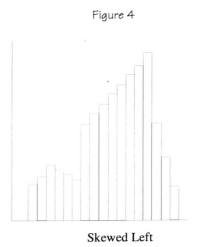

Skewed Left

Figure 5

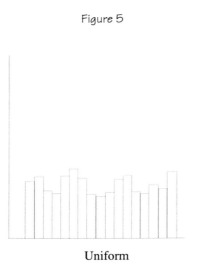

Uniform

Figure 6

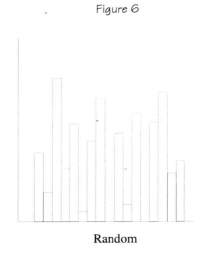

Random

The histogram example shown below would typically be considered a normal distribution. As more data points are collected, the bell shape will become more apparent.

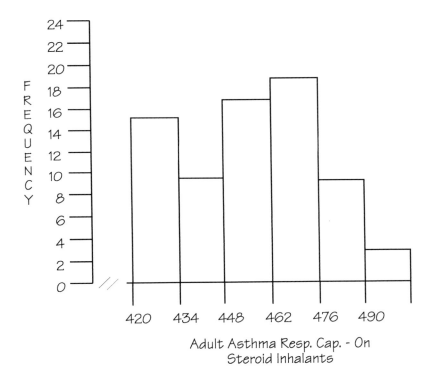

Adult Asthma Resp. Cap. - On
Steroid Inhalants

6. CALCULATE THE STATISTICS.

If you have a normally-shaped histogram, there are several statistics (numbers) which are useful to describe it. They are calculated to describe the area under the curve formed by the shape. The two most useful statistics are the central location and the spread.

a. Calculate the statistics for central location.

The central location of a set of data points is where (on what value) the middle of the data set is located. The central location is commonly described by the mean, the median, and/or the mode. The mean is the average of the data points. The symbol for the mean is $\overline{X}$. It is found by adding all the data points and dividing by the number of points.[1]

The **mean** for the example is:

$$\overline{X} = \frac{X_1 + X_2 + X_3 + \ldots + X_n}{n}$$

$$= \frac{430 + 420 + 440 + \ldots + 455}{69}$$

$$= \frac{31,460}{69}$$

$$= 455.94$$

The **median** ($\widetilde{X}$) is the middle number in the data set when the data points are arranged from low to high. Since there are 69 data points in the data set for the example, the median is the 35th point. The lowest point in the example is 420 and the highest is 500, so the median is:

$$\widetilde{X} = 420\ldots \ 455 \ \ldots 500$$

$$= 455$$

Note: If you have an even number of data points, the median is the average of the two middle points.

The **mode** is the value in the data set that occurs most often. For the example, 470 is the number that occurs most often, thus 470 is the mode for the data set.

---

[1] Recall that the mean for the X–R chart is found by averaging the subgroup means, and its symbol is $\overline{\overline{X}}$. When making a histogram, we are interested in the individual data points, not subgroup statistics.

b. **Calculate the statistic for spread.**

A statistic that describes the spread of the data set is the sample standard deviation. The standard deviation is a measure that tells us how different the values are from each other and from the middle (mean). The sample standard deviation (known as s) is tedious to calculate by hand. It is best to use a calculator or computer.

The steps to calculate the sample standard deviation are as follows:

1. Subtract the mean ($\overline{X}$) value from each individual value in the data set. Since there are 69 points in the data set, there will be 69 numbers after this step. The calculations for the first four data points are shown below.

$X - \overline{X}$ = 430 - 455.94 = - 25.94

420 - 455.94 = - 35.94

440 - 455.94 = - 15.94

460 - 455.94 = 4.06

2. Square each difference (answers from Step 1) to get rid of negative signs. If all the numbers were added, the positives would be canceled out by the negatives and the sum would be zero. To solve this, square all the answers from Step 1 to make them all positive. To square a number is to multiply it by itself. There will be 69 answers to this step when done. The first four data points are as follows:

$(X - \overline{X})^2$ = (-25.94) ^{2} = (-25.94)(-25.94) = 672.88

(-35.94) ^{2} = (-35.94)(-35.94) = 1291.68

(-15.94) ^{2} = (-15.94)(-15.94) = 254.08

(-4.06) ^{2} = (-4.06)(-4.06) = 16.48

3. Add the 69 squares of the differences from Step 2. The sum of the squares for the example is:

$\Sigma (X - \overline{X})^2$ = 672.88 + 1291.68 + 254.08 + 16.48 + ...

= 27,513.763

4. Divide the sum of the squares (the answer from Step 3) by one fewer than the number of points in the data set. There are 69 points in the data set so divide 27513.763 by 68.

$$\frac{\Sigma (X - \overline{X})^2}{n - 1} = \frac{27513.763}{68}$$

$$= 404.6142$$

5. Take the square root of the quotient (answer from Step 4) to get the sample standard deviation(s) for the data set.

$$s = \sqrt{404.6142}$$

$$= 20.12$$

The complete formula to find the sample standard deviation of a set of sample data is:

$$s = \sqrt{\frac{\Sigma (X - \overline{X})^2}{n - 1}}$$

7. COMPARE YOUR HISTOGRAM TO THE NORMAL DISTRIBUTION.

If the shape of your histogram is normal, it is useful to compare it to the normal distribution. Several characteristics of normal distributions will help in studying your histogram. The first characteristic of the normal distribution is that the mean (average), median, and mode are equal. The sketch below illustrates this idea.

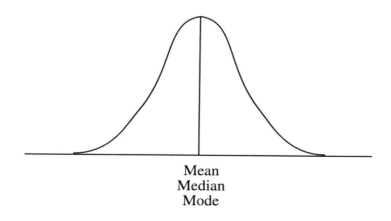

Mean
Median
Mode

A second characteristic of the normal distribution is that it is symmetrical. This means that if the distribution is cut in half, each side would be the mirror of the other. However, not all symmetrical shapes are normal; of the four shapes shown below, only D is normally distributed. The data must form a bell-shaped curve to be normal.

(A)

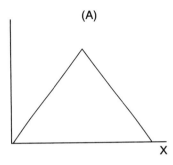

(B)

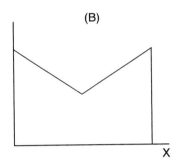

(C)

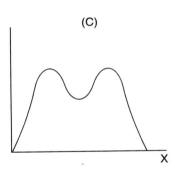

(D)

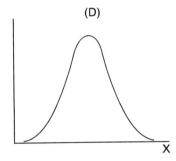

A third characteristic of the normal distribution is that the total area under the curve is equal to one. (To get the percentage of data under the curve, multiply 1 by 100 to get 100%.) The total area, however, is not shown. This is because the tails extend to infinity. Standard practice is to show 99.73% of the area, which is plus and minus 3 standard deviations from the average.

The fourth characteristic of the normal distribution is that the area under the curve can be determined. If we know the spread of the data (described by its standard deviation), we can determine the percentage of data under sections of the curve. To illustrate, refer to the sketches below. For curve A, 1 times the standard deviation to the right and 1 times the standard deviation to the left of the mean (the center of the curve) captures 68.26% of the area under the curve. For curve B, 2 times the standard deviation on either side of the mean captures 95.44% of the area under the curve. Consequently, for curve C, 3 times the standard deviation on either side of the mean captures 99.73% of the area under the curve. These percentages are true for all data that falls into a normally distributed pattern. These percentages are found in the Standard Normal Distribution Table (located in the Appendix).

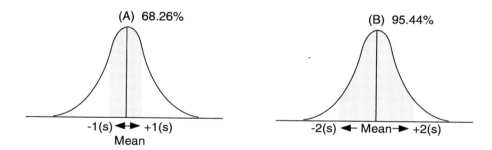

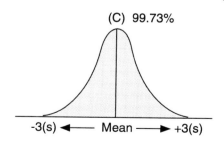

Once the mean and standard deviation of the data are known, the area under the curve can be described. For instance, 3 times the standard deviation on either side of the mean captures 99.73% of the data. The mean for the example is 455.94 and the standard deviation is 20.12, thus 3 x 20.12 on either side of the mean contains 99.73% of the data. (See the sketch below.)

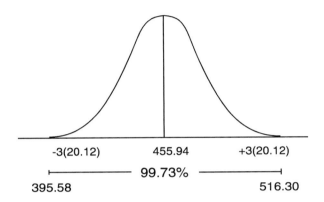

$$-3(20.12) \qquad 455.94 \qquad +3(20.12)$$

99.73%

395.58   516.30

☞ REMEMBER

1. A histogram is a picture of a set of data.

2. Only if the system is stable, can the histogram can be used to make predictions about the system.

3. The histogram shows the central location, shape, and spread of values sampled from the process.

GETTING THE MOST FROM HISTOGRAMS

Histograms provide three very important pieces of information about distributions of data values: shape, central location (the middle), and spread (how different the values are from each other and from the middle). Getting the most from this tool means being able to apply these statistical concepts.

Suppose the Hospital of Healthy Metropolis wants to know how to plan for telephone calls coming into the appointment center each day. The manager begins to collect daily data on incoming telephone calls to the appointment center, then checks stability with a c- control chart. By collecting data on daily totals, she can make a histogram to estimate the volume the center needs to be equipped to handle each day. The histogram is below.

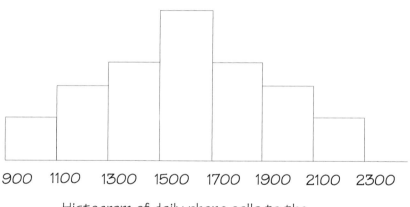

Histogram of daily phone calls to the
Appointment Center

The manager recognizes that her histogram looks symmetrical and reasonably bell-shaped. The shape indicates that most daily appointment phone calls cluster in the middle and tail off to the extremes.

Histograms show us how data can pile up; in any distribution of values, some values will occur more frequently than others. Those "piles" or peaks on the histogram show where there is similarity among the data. This is central location of the data, measured by the statistics mean, median, and mode. The manager can see that half the daily appointment calls are below and half above 1,600, the mean or average number of daily phone calls.

124

The manager does not have a complete picture, though, if she works only on the central location of the data. When she considers the spread of the data, she begins to see the extremes in the data and can plan accordingly. She calculates the standard deviation of the daily appointment center phone calls and finds it to be 200. Now the manager knows that only rarely will appointment center phone demand be less than 1,000 or more that 2,200 (± 3 standard deviations around 1600). Now she can calculate staffing needs, excess demand phone call roll-over plans, and equipment needs. If she had planned with only the central location in mind, she would have assured the hospital of unhappy customers.

Histograms of real data do not always turn out so neatly. Had the manager found a distribution with two peaks, one say at 1,100 and another at 1,800, she would have investigated to learn why this unusual pattern appeared. She might find, for instance, that the peak at 1,100 corresponded with weekend demand; the peak at 1,800 with Monday to Friday demand.

When histograms are used for **prediction**, it is extremely important to remember that the systems from which the data is drawn must be checked for stability. Unless the system is stable, the histogram taken at different times may be dramatically different in all three respects (central location, shape, and spread). A control chart is highly recommended for this test. Many managers have painful memories of histograms of initial samples that failed to predict the day-in and day-out performance of their process!

However, if the histogram is not to be used to make predictions, this condition for stability is not required. But **caution** should be taken. A histogram made today from an unstable system will indicate nothing about the system's performance tomorrow.

Histograms are useful on their own as predictive tools, but they are also used as part of a more detailed statistical analysis. Two such applications are testing for normality in X-MR charts and as the basis for capability analysis.

OTHER HEALTH CARE EXAMPLES

- Minutes waiting time prior to service (on phone, in reception prior to appointment, etc.)

- Cost per case (hysterectomy, CABG, etc.)

- Length of stay (by case for a particular DRG)

- Time to complete a type of lab test

- Length of time to respond to STAT requests from ED for radiology

- Number of sessions of therapy attended before premature termination of therapy

- Number of trips to ED per year for diabetics on preventive protocol versus diabetics not on preventive protocol

- Falls occurring in hospital by age of patient

- ED visits by time of day (24 one-hour increments)

- ED average patient waiting time by time of day (24 hour increments)

- Average hospital cafeteria lunch check

- Time to get through hospital cafeteria line from entrance to cashier by time of day (15 minute increments)

OPERATIONAL DEFINITION

OPERATIONAL DEFINITION

 WHAT IS IT?

An operational definition is a clear, concise, and detailed definition of a measure. Operational definitions allow people to understand their jobs with less confusion. Dr. Deming observed, "In the opinion of many people in industry there is nothing more important for transaction of business than use of operational definitions. It could also be said that no requirement of industry is so much neglected."[1] The goal of operational definitions is clear communication among everyone in the system. A good operational definition generates a question that yields a single yes or no answer, is consistently applied regardless of pressures of the moment, and is understandable.

The need for operational definitions is fundamental for all types of data but especially for attributes data where greater room for confusion exists. Imagine ten different medical records technicians having ten different ideas of what constitutes a complete inpatient medical record. Imagine the variation this situation causes in counting defective records (pass/fail). The data provided by these technicians is meaningless without an operational definition of a complete medical record that is understood and agreed upon by all. What does it mean to be "on-time" with a service? For instance, does "on-time" mean the service is delivered at exactly the promised time, or within a certain time period, perhaps no later than 15 minutes past the scheduled time? Fewer problems would occur if "on-time" were understood by customers and suppliers in the same way.

Although less ambiguous by nature, variables data must also be operationally defined. Operational definitions give meaning to variables by giving specific instruction on how they will be measured. For instance, what instrument should be used to measure time; a wall clock, a wrist watch, a stop watch? Should more than one clock, watch or stopwatch be used? Whose clock, watch or stopwatch will be used? To what degree of precision should time be kept— to the nearest five minutes, nearest minute, nearest half minute, to the second? When should the measurement be taken? When do we start to measure the time, and when do we stop? Even the simplest measurement can cause problems if specific directions have not been provided. No wonder it's difficult to measure late surgery starts, patient waiting time, surgical costs, etc.! Operational definitions are key to collecting useful data.

---

[1] W. Edwards Deming, *Out of the Crisis* (Cambridge: Massachusetts Institute of Technology, 1989, sixth printing), p. 276.

Operational definitions are used by anyone gathering data. All measures must be operationally defined before beginning data collection in order to get meaningful data.

 ## WHAT DOES IT LOOK LIKE?

Shown below is an example of a clear operational definition. A team in a hospital food service environment developed this operational definition before collecting data concerning late lunch carts.

1. **Characteristic of interest:** # of minutes each food cart varies from prescribed delivery time.

2. **Measuring instrument:** The observation will be made using the nursing unit wall clock on the unit to which the meal cart is delivered. Time will be recorded to the nearest minute.

3. **Method:** The Dietary Aide delivering the meal will record the number of minutes the lunch cart is over/under the prescribed delivery time by checking the nursing unit wall clock once the lunch cart has rolled to a stop in its assigned spot. This measurement will be taken: once a day, for each nursing unit food cart, M-F, for 2 weeks starting April 6.

4. **Decision criteria:** Each cart has an agreed-upon delivery time posted on cart. The Dietary Aide will note the actual delivery time on the check sheet. Comparing the actual delivery time to the agreed-upon delivery time, the Aide will note whether the cart is:

   - on time by annotating a 0 in the space provided

   - early by annotating a + and the number of minutes the cart was there before the agreed-upon delivery time

   - late by annotating a - and the number of minutes the cart was there past the agreed-upon delivery time

 ## WHEN IS IT USED?

Because the reliability of the baseline data collected early in an improvement project is crucial to the remaining steps in the project, **use operational definitions with every project when defining quality measures.** Any new measures added during the course of the project must also be operationally defined.

 ## How is it made?

1. Identify the characteristic of interest.

Identify the characteristic of interest associated with the project's quality measure(s). In the example, the project goal was to improve the on-time performance of the lunch cart delivery system. After understanding how it was performing in meeting prescribed delivery times, they set about identifying and measuring variables that would have an impact on timely meal delivery. The variables identified for study were:

- Started patient tray assembly line late
- Ran out of food item on the tray assembly line
- Short staffed (#)
- Inexperienced staff on shift
- Ran out of plate bases on tray assembly line
- Patient count over 400
- Incorrect diet tally
- More than 3 entrees on menu
- Trays incomplete—had to be corrected before loading
- Other

The next steps will show the operational definition created for "Started line late." Although the others are not developed here, the project team wrote operational definitions for all the variables of concern.

2. Select the measuring instrument.

Select the appropriate instrument for the variable of interest. In the example, the team is recording whether the line started on time or not. Because this variable deals with time, a clock is the appropriate measurement instrument.

Give any additional information related to the measuring instrument that may need to be clarified. For instance, in the example, the team stated:

- which clock would be used—the kitchen clock right above the patient tray line

• the measurement unit—round to the nearest minute

When measuring measurement data (time, money, height, weight, length, concentration) the measuring device is usually a tool such as a clock, a spectrometer, or calipers.

There is usually more clarifying information involved with measuring instruments for variables data. For instance, the working condition of the measuring instrument, how it should be held, in what type of light, number of decimal places in the recorded data, and so on. It is important to include as much additional information as necessary to make the use of the measuring instrument clear.

3. DESCRIBE THE TEST METHOD.

The test method is the actual procedure for taking the measurement. The test method includes the "where" and "how" of taking the measurement. In the example, the actual start time will be recorded by the patient tray line "Starter" at the start of each lunch patient tray line. The start of the tray line is signified when the first patient tray is placed on the line by the "Starter" and the moving tray belt is turned on. At this point the starter will record the actual start time on the data collection form and the number of trays to be produced at that lunch meal. After the meal period this time and tray count will be turned in to the shift leader who consolidates information on errors noted relating to all the variables under study onto the master data collection form.

4. STATE THE DECISION CRITERIA.

The judgment criteria are what allow teams to make a decision about the characteristic of interest. Does it exist or not? In this example, the decision criteria are as follows: the patient tray line lunch starting time is 11:00 AM if under 250 trays are to be made, and 10:45 AM if 250 trays or more are to be made that lunch period. The shift leader uses the actual start time, the tray count and this judgement criteria to determine whether the line started "on time" or not that day.

5. DOCUMENT THE OPERATIONAL DEFINITION.

It is important that the new operational definition be documented and standardized. Definitions should be included in training materials and job procedure sheets. The results of Steps 1 through 4 should be included in one document. Operational definitions can also be documented visually by providing physical samples that pass and fail the test. For example, patient trays that were deemed complete were displayed in the work area to assist food service personnel in identifying incomplete trays. A completed example for the operational definitions of "Started line late" is shown below:

1. **Characteristic of interest:** Variable = "Started line late" item measure is start time.

2. **Measuring instrument:** The kitchen clock right above the patient tray line will be used. The measurement unit is minutes rounded to the nearest minute.

3. **Method of test:** The actual start time will be recorded by the patient tray line "Starter" at the start of each lunch tray line. The start of the tray line is signified when the first patient tray is placed on the line by the "Starter" and the moving tray belt is turned on. At this point the starter will record the actual start time on the data collection form and the number of trays to be produced at that lunch meal. After the meal period, this time and tray count will be turned in to the shift leader who consolidates information onto the master data collection form about errors noted relating to all the variables under study.

4. **Decision criteria:** The patient tray line lunch starting time is 11:00 AM if under 250 patient trays are to be made, 10:45 AM if 250 trays or more are to be made that lunch period. The shift leader uses the actual start time, the tray count and this judgement criterion to determine if the line started "on time" or not that day and mark the master data collection form accordingly.

☞ REMEMBER

1. Operational definitions help reduce the variability in data collection so the data is more reliable.

2. Operational definitions are required for both attributes and variables data.

3. We need to use operational definitions to define quality measures before we gather data.

GETTING THE MOST FROM OPERATIONAL DEFINITIONS

Not only are operational definitions essential to establishing the measurement system, but they also provide an ongoing diagnostic tool. If a system appears to be changing, the cause may be a change in how operational definitions are being used. The control chart may show a process shift or intermittent special causes. This could be caused by new employees who haven't been properly trained or by some other change in the evaluation system. The evaluation system and operational definitions should be checked whenever a system is unstable to see if changes in the operational definition being used have occurred.

Operational definitions also provide an excellent communication tool for the supplier and customer. Agreeing on operational definitions is one way customers and suppliers can communicated more effectively and efficiently. What is a complete medical bill, a complete medical record? Clarifying these definitions can reduce errors, save time and make the job easier to perform.

OTHER HEALTH CARE EXAMPLES:

Operational definitions certainly require careful crafting between internal customers and suppliers. Input from the person actually using the operational definition is important. The definition should make jobs easier to perform. Each person using the definition should produce the same result. If results vary, the operational definition should be revised to clear up any portions that are causing confusion.

Operational definitions between the health care organization (supplier) and the patient or payer (customer and stakeholder) can be even more complex. For example, what is a complication? In reviewing a recent data collection form from a health care regulator, the results of which can influence hospital financing, the following operational definition was noted:

- **Cardiovascular Outcomes and Complications:** Significant vascular complications: aortic dissection, iliac/femoral dissection, arterial embolus requiring treatment, etc.

- **So what does "etc." mean?** Will various hospitals respond to the regulator the same way? If more complications reduce the chance the hospital will get a contract, or changes their reimbursement rates, how many hospitals will have any "etc."?

- **What is a "good" clinical outcome related to same-day GYN surgery?**
  From the perspective of several surgeons, the operational definition
  consisted of complication rates, mortality rates, etc. The patients, however,
  defined good outcome as "feeling better," "returning to work quickly," and
  as a "caring experience." Developing operational definitions between
  patients and health care suppliers requires great collaboration. Patients can
  not typically define the technically clinical portions of the operational
  definitions. Skilled clinical subject matter experts must do this. However,
  clinical subject matter experts alone cannot completely operationally
  define "good outcome" from the patient, payer, or regulator perspective.
  Some of these large, rather complex, operational definitions used in health
  care may require a number of dimensions of quality to be operationally
  defined in order to be useful. Technical clinical quality dimensions, patient
  functioning, customer satisfaction, and cost may all need to be addressed
  before "good outcome" for clinical care can be operationally defined.

PARETO DIAGRAM

PARETO DIAGRAM

WHAT IS IT?

A Pareto diagram is a simple bar chart which ranks related measures in decreasing order of occurrence. The principle was first developed by Vilfredo Pareto, an Italian economist and sociologist who conducted a study in Europe in the early 1900s on wealth and poverty. Pareto found that wealth was concentrated in the hands of the few and poverty in the hands of the many. Pareto's principle was named and popularized by Joseph M. Juran in the late 1940s. Juran was searching for a name for his studies on the maldistribution of quality losses and came up with Pareto's earlier study. It was Juran who made the principle a universal concept. The principle is based on the unequal distribution of things in the universe. It is the law of the "significant few versus the trivial many." The significant few things will generally make up 80% of the whole, while the trivial many will make up about 20%.

The purpose of a Pareto diagram is to separate the significant aspects of a problem from the trivial ones. By graphically separating the aspects of a problem, a team will know where to direct its improvement efforts. Reducing the largest bars identified in the diagram will do more for overall improvement than reducing the smaller ones.

An improvement team can use a Pareto diagram many times during an improvement project. It is one of the most useful analytic tools. A team uses a Pareto diagram to analyze causes, study results, and plan for continuous improvement. A team first uses the Pareto diagram to stratify (divide) data to identify the most significant aspects of a problem. The team can then generate theories for improvement to reduce the significant aspects. After trying its improvement theories, the team may make a new Pareto diagram to see if the theories have worked. If the theories have worked, what had previously been the largest bars will be smaller. For continuous improvement, the team uses the new diagram to make plans to reduce the "new" largest bars.

136

⟳ WHAT DOES IT LOOK LIKE?

An example of a Pareto diagram is shown below. This diagram represents events that could be causing delays in getting open heart patients from the surgical suite to the CICU for post surgical monitoring. The cardiac care team used this diagram to identify the type of delaying events happening most frequently.

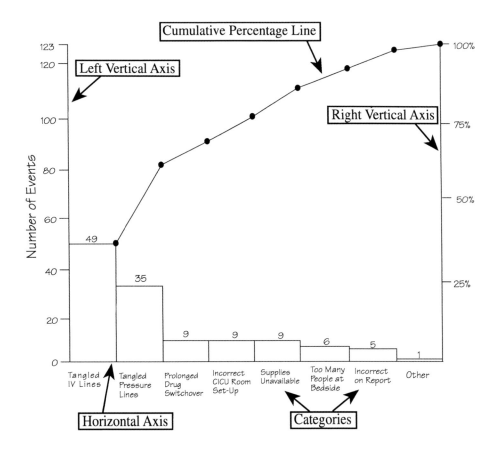

 WHEN IS IT USED?

Use a Pareto diagram when you can answer "yes" to both these questions:

1. **Can data be arranged into categories?** Categories are "points of view."[1] Points of view are ways of looking at the data: by time, location, type, or symptom (i.e. Unit 3 West, 2 East, etc. or MDC, DRG, procedure, etc.)

2. **Is the rank of each category important?** Having limited resources, the team should always work on the most important problems and the most important causes. The rank of categories on Pareto diagrams guides teams to efficient and effective work.

 HOW IS IT MADE?

These steps assume that the problem for analysis has been chosen as a result of brainstorming or by using existing data. The measurement unit, such as number, time, or cost, has also been chosen. In the example, the measurement unit is number of delaying events.

1. SELECT LOGICAL CATEGORIES FOR THE IDENTIFIED TOPIC OF ANALYSIS.

Data can be divided into categories by time, location, type, or symptom. In the example, the topic being studied is "delays in open heart patient transport from OR to CICU." The team had chosen to categorize the data by type of delay observed. Members of the team who understand the transfer process have chosen the types of delays, based on their experience.

Sometimes the category types may not be apparent. In this case, data can be collected and organized into categories afterward. For instance, in our process improvement study, the nurse can make a record of the type of delay he or she experienced in transferring the patient. At the end of the collection period, all the like items are grouped together to form categories and are named. For example, "ventilator in wrong place" and monitoring equipment in wrong position" could both be grouped under "room set-up wrong." The number of categories should be limited to 10 or fewer. An "other" category is always a good idea just in case the team missed a source of delay in its initial brainstorming.

---

[1] Histoshi Kume, *Statistical Methods for Quality Improvement* (Tokyo, Japan: The Association for Overseas Technical Scholarship, 1988), p.28.

2. Specify the time period.

Specify the time period in which the data will be collected. The time period depends on the situation being analyzed. In this example, the time period is one month because the clinical team believed that all types of unanticipated delays occur in any given month. If only a week were chosen, the Pareto diagram might not accurately represent the data.

3. Collect the data.

Collect the data by category for the specified time period. A check sheet is best to use for collecting the data. Make a check sheet with the category names listed along the left side and space to the right of each to make tally marks. Each time there is an occurrence, make a tally mark in the space to the right of the appropriate category. At the end of the time period, total the tally marks to the right. A completed check sheet for the example is shown below.

Category	Hours of Delay	Total
prolonged drug switchover	𝍸 IIII	9
incorrect on report	𝍸	5
tangled IV lines	𝍸𝍸𝍸𝍸𝍸𝍸𝍸𝍸𝍸 IIII	49
tangled presssure lines	𝍸𝍸𝍸𝍸𝍸𝍸𝍸	35
incorrect CICU room set-up	𝍸 IIII	9
supplies unavailable	𝍸 IIII	9
too many people at bedside	𝍸 I	6
other	I	1
		123

4. CONSTRUCT A FREQUENCY TABLE.

Construct a frequency table from the check sheet data. A frequency table lists the categories in decreasing rank order on the left. The table has column titles across the top labeled "Frequency" and "Cumulative Frequency." (The "other" category is always listed at the bottom of the frequency table.) In the example, the frequency table would begin as follows:

	Frequency	Cumulative Frequency
tangled IV lines	49	
tangled pressure lines	35	
prolonged drug switchover	9	
incorrect CICU room set-up	9	
supplies unavailable	9	
too many people at bedside	6	
incorrect on report	5	
other	1	
	123	

The cumulative frequency for any category is the number of occurrences in the category plus all frequencies in categories above it. The cumulative frequency through "tangled pressure lines" is 35 + 49 = 84.

The cumulative frequency through "prolonged drug switchover" is 9 + 35 + 49 = 93.

Calculate the cumulative frequency for each category. The completed frequency table for the example is shown below.

	Frequency	Cumulative Frequency
tangled IV lines	49	49
tangled pressure lines	35	84
prolonged drug switchover	9	93
incorrect CICU room set-up	9	102
supplies unavailable	9	111
too many people at bedside	6	117
incorrect on report	5	122
other	1	123
	123	

5. DRAW AND SCALE THE HORIZONTAL AND VERTICAL AXES.

a. Draw a horizontal axis.

The length of the horizontal axis (x-axis) depends on the size of the graph one wants to make. Draw the horizontal axis to the length which will provide the best picture of the data. This could vary from very small (say, two inches or less) to a full-page width (six or seven inches).

b. Decide on the scaling factor for the horizontal axis.

The scaling factor for the x-axis is the width of each bar. Divide the horizontal axis into the same number of equal parts as there are categories. When using graph paper to draw the Pareto, make each category the same number of squares in width. In the example below, the horizontal axis is divided into eight equal parts for the eight categories.

c. Draw the vertical axes.

Draw two vertical axes of equal height, one at each end of the horizontal axis. Make these vertical lines at least as long as the horizontal line. (If the bars are tall, these vertical lines may need to be extended.) An example of the horizontal and vertical axes is shown below. Label the left vertical axis with the units of measurement such as frequency (number of events, occurrences), hours, etc.

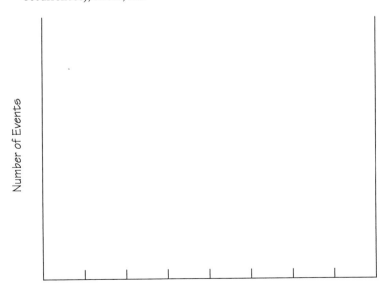

d. Scale the vertical axes.

Scale (divide) the left axis to provide convenient markers to measure the height of the bars. This axis should start at the bottom with zero and should be scaled appropriately to include, near the top, the value of the total cumulative frequency from Step 4 (123 for the example). The dividing markers should be labeled with multiples of easy-to-work-with numbers such as 5, 10, or 20. In the example, each marker increases by 20 as one goes up the left axis.

The right vertical axis is labeled with percentages so that a cumulative percentage line can be drawn in later. Begin by labeling a marker as 100% on the right axis directly across from the value of the total cumulative frequency from Step 4 (123 for the example). Next, divide the right axis into four equal sections and label the remaining markers 25%, 50%, and 75%. The example completed through this step is shown below.

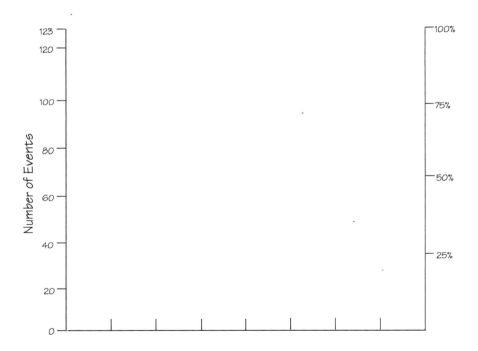

6. DRAW AND LABEL THE BARS FOR EACH CATEGORY.

Draw each bar to the height corresponding to its frequency (from the frequency table in Step 4) and the width to the predetermined scale. The bars should touch one another. (If there is an "Other" category, it will be the last bar on the right, regardless of its height.) Over the top of each bar, write the value corresponding to its frequency. Label each bar under the horizontal axis. The bars may be shaded for emphasis. The example completed through this step is shown below.

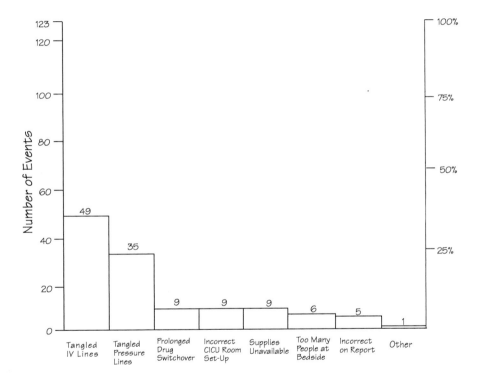

7. DRAW IN THE CUMULATIVE PERCENTAGE LINE.

Draw a cumulative percentage line on the Pareto diagram so that the cumulative percentage for each bar can be read from the right vertical axis. The cumulative frequency for each category (bar) is plotted to make the cumulative percentage line.

Refer to the frequency table in Step 4 for the information to draw the cumulative percentage line. Make a dot over the upper right corner of each bar that corresponds to its cumulative frequency from the table. For instance, the cumulative frequency for "Tangled IV Lines" is 49, so make a dot that corresponds to 49 (on the left vertical axis) above the upper right corner of the first bar. The cumulative frequency for "Tangled Pressure Lines" is 84. Make a dot that corresponds to 84 (on the left vertical axis) above the upper right corner of the second bar. The example completed through these first two bars is shown below.

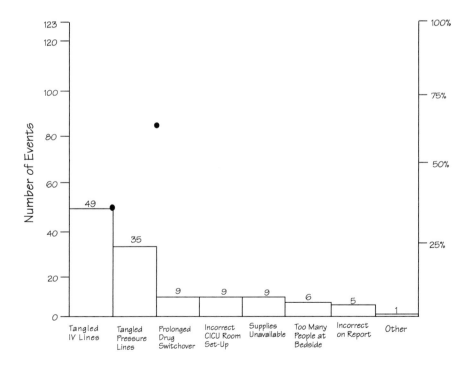

Continue plotting the cumulative frequencies for the remaining categories. The dot for the last category should be at the 100% mark on the right vertical axis. Draw the cumulative percentage line by connecting the dots. The completed example is shown below.

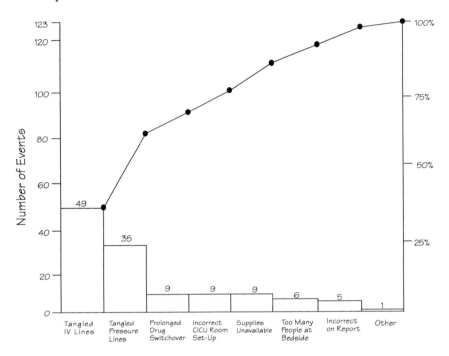

8. REVIEW THE RESULTS OF THE PARETO.

Look at the chart to identify the categories that are significant compared to those that are trivial. Expect the significant few categories to make up approximately 80% of the data in the Pareto diagram. This can be tested by looking at the cumulative percentage line. In the example, "Tangled IV Lines" and "Tangled Pressure Lines" are the two largest bars. Reading from the right axis, they make up roughly 70% of the data. This means that out of all the causes of open heart patient transfer delays, these two categories have occurred most often, causing about 70% of the delays.

Be careful, however, because the "significant few-trivial many" principle does not always hold. No matter how data is categorized, it can be ranked and made into a Pareto diagram. Sometimes no single bar is dramatically different from the others, and the Pareto looks either flat or gently sloping. To attack the tall bar in that situation is to no advantage. In the example, there is a substantial difference between the first two and the remaining bars, just as one would expect.

 **REMEMBER**

1. A Pareto diagram is a bar chart that ranks data by categories.

2. Use of the Pareto diagram is based on the idea that only a few categories contain most of the data.

3. We can do the most for overall improvement by directing efforts toward the few largest categories (bars) identified.

4. We can use a Pareto diagram for several purposes during an improvement project: to analyze causes, to study results, and to plan for continuous improvement.

5. The Pareto diagram is a simple but powerful analytical tool.

 GETTING THE MOST FROM PARETO ANALYSIS

Despite its simplicity, Pareto analysis is one of the most powerful of the problem-solving tools for system improvement. Getting the most from Pareto analysis includes making subdivisions, making multi-perspective analyses, and making repeat analyses.

Subdivisions are useful when data has been first recorded at a very general level, but problem solving needs to occur at a more specific level. A health care system made a Pareto chart of each of its member hospitals' rates of unplanned readmissions within 31 days of discharge. Once a hospital has identified what contributes most to unplanned readmissions, the next step might be to analyze that hospital's unplanned readmissions by Major Diagnostic Code (MDC). If MDC 4, Respiratory System, turned up as the biggest category of unplanned readmissions for a hospital in question, yet another Pareto of unplanned readmissions within MDC 4 might reveal which Diagnostic Related Group (DRG) was involved most frequently in unplanned readmissions. Because the Pareto principle holds for subgroupings of data, such successive analyses can be performed to help target small elements of a large problem. An illustration of this use of Pareto analysis is shown on the following page.

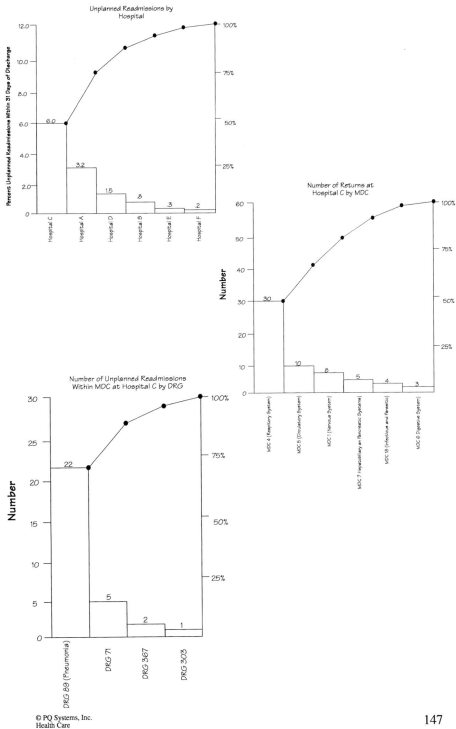

Unplanned Readmissions by Hospital

Number of Returns at Hospital C by MDC

Number of Unplanned Readmissions Within MDC at Hospital C by DRG

Multi-perspective analyses are useful when data can be stratified or subdivided in several different ways. The health care professional might study unplanned readmissions by DRG volume or by cost to the health care system. A hospital may find that DRG 89, pneumonia, may have accounted for the greatest volume of unplanned readmissions over a period of time, but that DRG 423, Infectious Process, specifically related to DRG 209, multiple joint replacement, accounts for the majority of costs. Depending on priority, the problem could be attacked to reduce either the highest frequency, or the highest cost source of unplanned readmissions. The health care manager might study hospital unplanned readmissions by service, procedure, organism, health care provider, patient socio-economic status or by any other set of categories he or she thinks may reveal opportunities for improvement. Multi-perspective Pareto analysis helps assure that a set of data is reviewed from all angles and that many explanations for variability are considered. An example of this use of Pareto analysis is shown below.

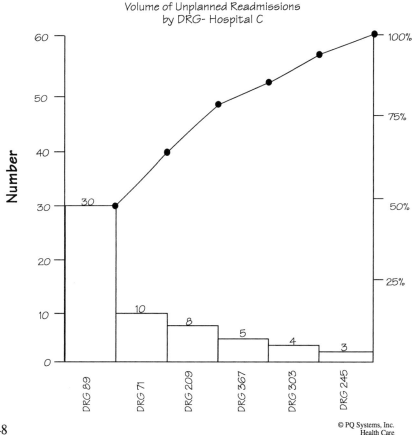

Volume of Unplanned Readmissions by DRG- Hospital C

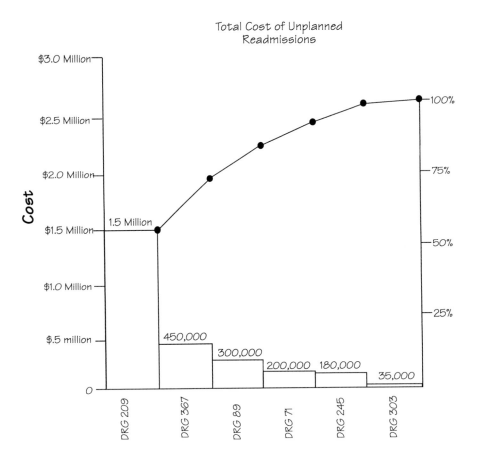

Total Cost of Unplanned
Readmissions

Repeat analyses are useful when improvement activity is underway and performance data is changing over time. If the health care manager is working with their staff to reduce the number of high cost unplanned readmissions in DRG 209, he or she might repeat an earlier Pareto analysis using more recent data to see if the target category has shrunk. Depending on the cycle of data collection—hourly, daily, weekly, monthly, quarterly, or other—repeated Pareto analyses help to monitor the improvements made to the system producing the data. An example of this use of Pareto analysis is shown on the following two pages.

Pareto Diagram

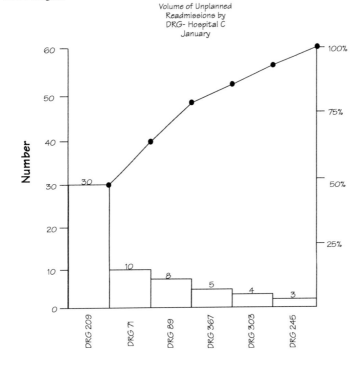

Volume of Unplanned
Readmissions by
DRG- Hospital C
January

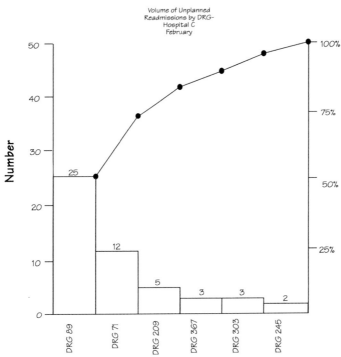

Volume of Unplanned
Readmissions by DRG-
Hospital C
February

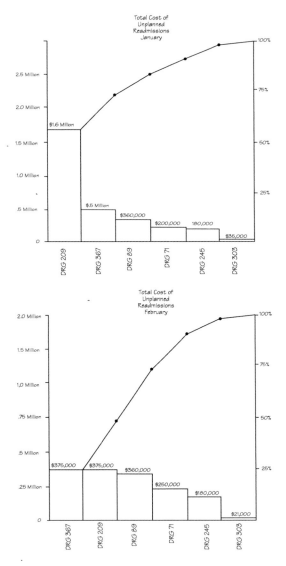

Total Cost of Unplanned Readmissions January

Total Cost of Unplanned Readmissions February

Caution is in order for users of Pareto analysis who have not monitored the systems they are studying for stability. A wildly fluctuating system will produce inconsistent Pareto rankings that can lead to misjudgments. Suppose the health care manager failed to note that the source of unplanned readmissions varied greatly from month to month. If he or she chooses a month in which unplanned readmissions were unusually high for the analysis, the ranking of categories may be entirely different from those of a month in which unplanned readmission were unusually low.

OTHER HEALTH CARE EXAMPLES

Some of the areas in which health care professionals have used Pareto charts include:

- Patient satisfaction & dissatisfaction, what were biggest satisfiers, dissatisfiers?

- Inpatient falls occurring by unit

- Number of inpatient falls occurring by DRG

- Reasons for Monday phone calls to the outpatient Primary Care Clinic

- Causes of medication errors

- Causes of adverse drug reactions

- Reasons for delays (in treatment, in surgery, in discharge, etc.)

- Sources of referrals to home care

- Hospitals with most unplanned C-sections

- Reasons for same day surgery cancellations

- What customers called their HMO about most often (what benefits)

- Reasons for patients switching to a new physician

- Sources of cost in treating a category of patients (DRG) (e.g. OR cost, medication cost, supplies)

- DRGs with the greatest gap between charges and reimbursements

RUN CHART

RUN CHART

WHAT IS IT?

A run chart is a line graph of data plotted over time. The plotted data can be variables (measurements) or attributes (counts) data.

The purpose of making a run chart is to look at a system's behavior over time. By collecting data over time, trends or patterns in the data can be detected, if they exist. For instance, assume a run chart is made with data collected from the X-ray process documenting retakes per week. The data reveals the process drifts upward toward the end of every week. Armed with this information, the technicians can study the process and variables resulting in high number of retakes at the end of each week, change the process, and continue to collect and chart the data to test the effect of their change. This same data lumped together and put into a histogram would not have revealed this important information. A histogram is only a snapshot of the process; a run chart is more like a movie, showing the process as it develops over time.

A run chart is used when we are gathering baseline data at the beginning of a project. The run chart used alone can often reveal very important information, but the chart is usually taken a step further and made into a control chart by adding control limits to assess system stability.

WHAT DOES IT LOOK LIKE?

An example of a completed run chart is shown below. A team of providers and support staff in a Radiology Department made this run chart to analyze radiology retakes per week.

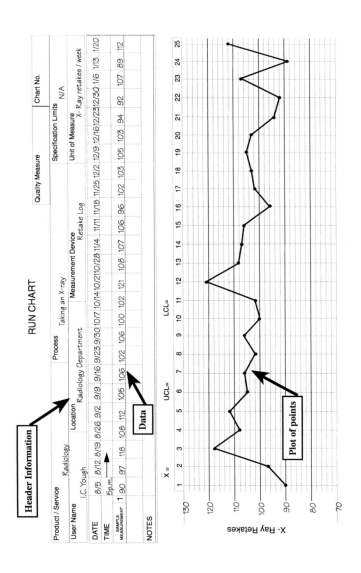

WHEN IS IT USED?

Use a run chart when you can answer "yes" to both these questions:

1. **Is data, either variables or attributes, collected over time?** A run chart can be constructed from variables or attributes data as long as the data is taken as the system operates.

2. **Is the time order of the data preserved?** Since a run chart is used to look at the behavior of the system over time, it is critical that the data is recorded in the order it is collected and produced. Mixing the order of samples would be like editing a film with no attention to the sequence of events.

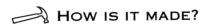

HOW IS IT MADE?

These steps assume that the data for constructing the run chart has already been collected and recorded on a data collection sheet or control chart paper. Twenty-five data points or more are desirable. It is important that the data collector make note of any changes or unusual occurrences in the process during data collection. This will become important later to identify causes of unusual patterns on the run chart.

1. COMPLETE THE HEADER INFORMATION.

Before entering the data, complete the header information for the chart. If control chart paper is used, as in the example, fill in the area at the top of the paper. If regular grid paper is used, title the chart including the product/service, process, location, quality measure, date, and anything else important to the context of the chart.

2. RECORD THE DATA.

If control chart paper is used to make the run chart, enter the collected data in the data entry section of the chart, if it was not originally recorded there. The data must be entered in the order in which it has been collected. A simple run chart is usually constructed from a set of individual readings; however, some control chart paper has space for larger subgroups. The example with completed header information and recorded data is shown on the following page.

RUN CHART   Quality Measure

Product / Service		Process		Specifi.
Radiology		Taking an X-ray		

User Name		Location		Measurement Device		Unit of M
I.C. Yough		Radiology Department		Retake Log		

DATE		8/5	8/12	8/19	8/26	9/2	9/9	9/16	9/23	9/30	10/7	10/14	10/21	10/28	11/4	11/11	11/18	11/25	12/2	12/9	12
TIME		5p.m.																			
SAMPLE MEASUREMENT	1	90	97	118	108	112	105	106	102	106	100	102	121	108	107	106	96	102	103	105	
MOVING RANGE, M R																					
NOTES																					

X =   UCL=   LCL=

INDIVIDUALS

1 2 3 4 5 6 7 8 9 10 11 12 13 14 15 16 17

3. DETERMINE THE SCALING FOR THE CHART.

The procedure for scaling the chart depends on the type of data being charted, variables or attributes. Follow Step (a) below for variables data and Step (b) for attributes data.

Run charts can be plotted on any grid paper, including either standard graph paper or control chart paper. The type of paper is immaterial to the process of scaling and plotting. These steps assume use of control chart paper. (Note: Ignore the space for recording the ranges and use only the top chart.)

a. Scaling for variables data.

Begin by finding the largest and smallest values in the data set. Subtract the smaller value from the larger. In the example the largest data value is 121 and the smallest is 89, so their difference is 121 - 89 = 32.

Next, divide the answer (32) by two-thirds of the number of lines available on the chart paper to get the increment value for one line. Use only two-thirds of the number of lines available to allow space to plot shifts in the future. On the control chart paper being used, there are 30 lines, so divide the difference from above by 20 (two-thirds) to find the increment value for one line on the chart.

$$\text{Increment Value} = \frac{32}{20} = 1.6$$

The increment value may be rounded to an easier-to-work-with number. However, it should always be rounded upward. In this case, we will round 1.6 to 2.

Start numbering the lines from the center of the chart. But first find the number that will mark the center. Since the values range from 89 to 121 in the example, label the center of the chart with the number that is approximately halfway between 89 and 121. To find this number, add half the range (the highest value minus the lowest value) to the lowest value. The range found earlier is 32 (121 - 89 = 32). Half of 32 is 16, so add 16 to 89 to get the center number.

The center number is:

$$89 + 16 = \textbf{105.}$$

Find the center dark reference line on the chart and locate 105 near it in such a way that you can label the center line with a number easy to work with. In this case, 100 is a good number, so label the center dark reference line 100. To number the remaining lines, add the increment value found earlier, 2, to each line moving away from 100, above and below. Label each dark reference line with its value. The example completed through this step is shown below.

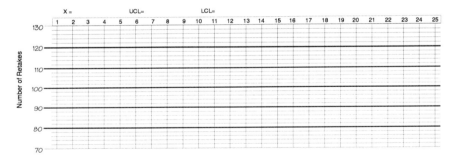

b. **Scaling for attributes data.**

Run charts for attributes data are scaled using the same procedure as for variables data with two exceptions: (1) Locate only the largest value in the data set. That is the number to be divided by two-thirds of the number of lines available. (2) When numbering the lines on the chart, start at the bottom of the chart on the first line with 0 and add the increment value to each line as you move upward. Label every dark reference line (usually every fifth line).

4. PLOT THE VALUES ON THE CHART.

Starting with the first data point, plot each point on the chart. On the control chart paper are vertical lines to act as guides for plotting the points. It is important that the points are plotted in the order in which they have been collected. Connect the plotted points (dots) with straight lines. The example completed through this step is shown below.

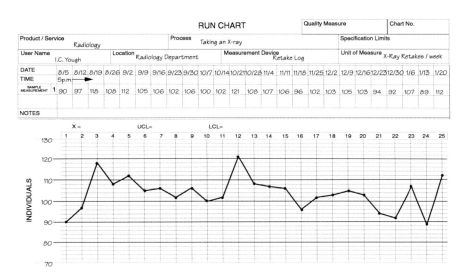

5. INTERPRET THE CHART.

a. Look for runs.

If you find seven points in a row rising or falling, you have found an unusual circumstance that calls for investigation. Finding evidence of a run is neither good or bad. It simply raises a flag that says, "Ask why."

b. Look for other nonrandom patterns.

You may find a repeating pattern that corresponds to the order of the data. Weekly counts of X-Ray retakes in the Radiology Department may produce a chart with spikes corresponding to the dates of recalibration. Upon investigation, you may find technicians have been gradually adjusting their technique to account for machine calibration changes. When machines are recalibrated, the adjustments made previously now result in errors and retakes. Staff could investigate calibration frequency, staff notification of calibration, and other variables to reduce retake spikes.

Similarly, valleys may correspond to another day of the week because of technician assignment, machine used, etc. Any nonrandom or repeating pattern is cause for investigation.

If you find no unusual patterns, you may observe how different the readings are from each other. Do they swing wildly from highs to lows or are they quite similar to each other? Further analysis by control chart is the next likely step.

In the example, there are no runs or nonrandom patterns. Only one point (number 12) stands out from the others and may be cause for further investigation. However, without completing a control chart for the data, there is no way of knowing whether this point is really unusual or one that could be expected from this system.

 REMEMBER

1. A run chart is a plot of data over time.

2. Time is plotted on the horizontal axis and the variable value is plotted on the vertical axis.

3. A run chart is used to detect trends or patterns in data over time.

4. A run chart is the basis for a control chart.

GETTING THE MOST FROM RUN CHARTS

Run charts are one of the simplest statistical tools, yet they provide a great deal of information. They should be used often and with different kinds of data. They can be easily constructed, so they are especially useful for one-time analyses of historical data.

It is useful to display run charts for staff members to view. A department or group in a hospital may plot daily, weekly, monthly or other periodic measures and post these for all to see. Number of patients seen in a day, patient waiting times, or medical supply dollars expensed are often plotted in this way. But many other consolidated figures could benefit from the same method. Patterns and trends are much easier to see on a chart than in a matrix of rows and columns. People are drawn to a graphic more than to text or lists of figures, so run charts are an attractive alternative to these other displays or summary reports.

Run charts should be used as a quick test of the performance of a system. When you begin to plot data over time in this fashion, it may take you longer to obtain enough data points for conventional control chart analysis. Yet this data is fine for a run chart. Throughput data (total numbers of patients seen, total dollars spent per day or specific period) should be plotted immediately on a run chart to enable quick diagnosis of system changes over time or to identify signs that the process has begun to stabilize.

 ## OTHER HEALTH CARE EXAMPLES:

- LOS for specific DRG

- Cost per case by provider

- Waiting time by specific time of day or day of week

- Consults per week by diagnosis or by provider or both

- Time is takes to transfer a patient

- Time in hours or minutes to clean a patient room (turnaround time)

- Time to admit patient

- Errors per patient bill

- Time from diagnosis to treatment

- Time in hours to obtain a STAT consult

- Time in days to obtain a consultation

- Monitoring surgery waiting times

- Time in days to first diabetic appointment

- Average weekly inpatient satisfaction

- Pharmacy waiting time

- Time to complete meds

- Lab turn around time: ETC urinalysis TAT (min)

- Surgical start time delays (min)

- Unplanned readmissions (by percent or by percent to a benchmark)

SAMPLING

SAMPLING

WHAT IS IT?

Sampling is a tool that guides the quantitative study of a system. Perhaps the best way to understand sampling is with an illustration.

Imagine a loaf of bread in front of you. If you want to know how good the bread is, would you eat the whole loaf? No, of course not. To make a judgment about the entire loaf, you need only to taste or **sample** the loaf. You might think of eating a slice. The term **sample** describes the slice and the term **population** describes the loaf. A sample, then, is a subset of the population collected to make an estimate of the population being studied.

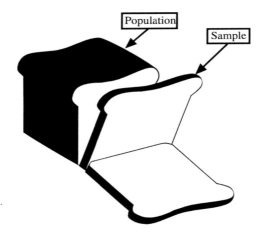

Now imagine you work in a bakery. A population in which you might now be interested is all the bread you have made today. A sample size of one slice from one loaf does not make sense for this larger population. Perhaps the sample would become several loaves of bread taken at different times throughout the day. So you see, the sample is relative to the population you want to study.

But how can you talk about the bread you made yesterday, the bread you made today, and the bread you will make tomorrow? Working to improve quality involves examining ongoing processes. It is impossible to get what a process produced in the past and will produce in the future into one place. You can get your mind around it but not your hands. So, in sampling, sample from an ongoing process. Use that data to make judgments about a **conceptual population**. See the figure below.

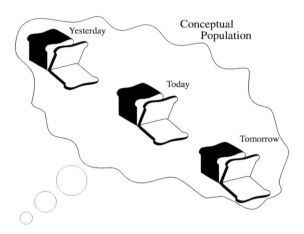

Suppose that in the ongoing process of making bread, you are interested in the weight of the loaf. You would not want to weigh every single loaf you make because this would be too expensive, too time consuming, and no more accurate than sampling some of the loaves. Sampling for quality improvement is a matter of taking small samples frequently over time. But the questions now become (1) how many loaves do you weigh each time you take a sample, and (2) how often do you take a sample? These two questions, how much and how often, get to the heart of sampling. You'll learn how to answer these questions in the "How is it made?" section.

We also use sampling to guide our data collection. Imagine a clinical improvement team working on improving the process of completing STAT lab requests from the inpatient units, surgeries, the Emergency Department, and the outpatient clinics. One key quality measure might be the turn around time (TAT), or the time from when a STAT lab is ordered to the time the results are logged into the computer. It would be very time consuming to measure and record the TAT for every single STAT order, especially in a large medical center. So the team would want to sample a few orders at a specified time interval over time and record the TATs.

Clinical improvement teams first use sampling prior to data gathering at the beginning of the project. They continue using it throughout the project as they check the success of their data collection and the need to collect new data.

~⊙⊙ WHAT DOES IT LOOK LIKE?

Because sampling is a mental process of deciding how much data to gather and how often to gather it, it is difficult to show a picture of it. However, the output from the decisions is recorded on a form called a "data gathering plan," which is possible to show. The following are two data gathering plans from two clinical improvement projects in a health care system.

This first data gathering form is from a clinical improvement team working to improve the average STAT lab turnaround time (TAT). The quality measure is: the time it takes to complete each STAT lab request. The time it takes to get STAT lab results can impact crucial patient care decisions.

DATA GATHERING PLAN

WHAT DATA	HOW	HOW MUCH	HOW OFTEN	WHERE	METHODS	WHO
Measure #1: _# Times in minutes per STAT lab_ Operational Definition						
Time in minutes for STAT Lab completion	Determine time between order entry in computer and results entry in computer to nearest minute	Sample of 5 STAT lab (TAT)	Each Day, Monday- Sunday for 1 week at 8 am, 12 noon, 4 pm, 8 pm, and 12 midnight	From inpatient units	Select the first 5 STAT labs requested after the stated collection time and note the minutes it took to complete each	Lab Technician
Time:						
Location:						
Symptom:						
Type:						
Measure #2: _____ Operational Definition						
Time:						
Location:						
Symptom:						
Type:						

The second data gathering sheet was made by an individual trying to decrease the number of errors on medical bills. The quality measure is number of errors per bill at time of patient discharge from the hospital.

DATA GATHERING PLAN

WHAT DATA	HOW	HOW MUCH	HOW OFTEN	WHERE	METHODS	WHO
Measure #1: **Errors per Bill** Operational Definition						
	Record the number of errors per medical bill at time of discharge.	5 bills per day for each of three clerks	Daily 8 am for the previous day, Monday through Friday for 2 weeks	Billing office	Select every 5th bill completed the previous day by each clerk.	Billing Supervisor
Time:						
Location:						
Symptom:						
Type:						
Measure #2: _____ Operational Definition						
Time:						
Location:						
Symptom:						
Type:						

When is it used?

Sampling is used any time data is to be gathered. Data cannot be gathered until sample size (how much) and sample frequency (how often) are determined, even if you plan to collect data on every item in the process (100 percent coverage).

 # How is it made?

These steps assume that the system to be improved has been described, a flow chart has been done, and the data to be gathered has been determined and operationally defined.

1. **DETERMINE WHAT QUESTION YOU ARE ASKING OF THE DATA.**

   Before you can collect any data, you must clearly understand and define what you want to know from the data. There are several questions you can ask about any group of data. Let's look at the data below for an example.

Errors on Medical Bills (per subgroup of 5 bills/day for each clerk)

Billing Clerk	M	T	W	TH	F	M	T	W	TH	F
				Days						
A	3	4	3	6	9	2	5	3	4	7
B	5	8	4	7	12	6	4	9	3	11
C	3	2	1	3	5	1	2	1	2	7

The data shows the number of billing errors per subgroup of 5 bills by each clerk in a given health care system. There are several questions you might ask about this data. First, you might want to know if there is any difference among daily results (a representation of the system). In this case, you would group clerk A, B, and C's results, and plot one point for each day. You have 10 samples (or points). See the figure below.

Days

Billing Clerk	M	T	W	TH	F	M	T	W	TH	F
A	3	4	3	6	9	2	5	3	4	7
B	5	8	4	7	12	6	4	9	3	11
C	3	2	1	3	5	1	2	1	2	7
Total	11	14	8	16	26	9	11	13	9	25

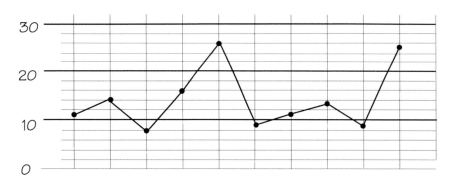

A second question is how the data generated by each clerk might differ. To answer this question, organize the data by clerk for each day of the week.

In this case, the sample (or subgroup) size would be 5 bills per clerk and would have 10 samples (or points) as shown below for clerk B.

Days

Billing Clerk	M	T	W	TH	F	M	T	W	TH	F	Avg.
A	3	4	3	6	9	2	5	3	4	7	4.6
B	5	8	4	7	12	6	4	9	3	11	6.9
C	3	2	1	3	5	1	2	1	2	7	2.7

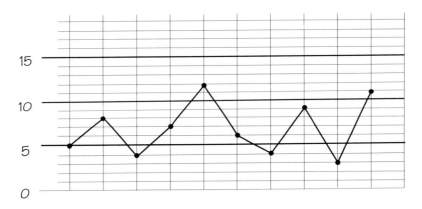

2. DETERMINE THE FREQUENCY (HOW OFTEN) OF SAMPLING.

The frequency of sampling means how often a sample should be taken. A sample should be taken at least as often as the process is expected to change. Examine all factors which are expected to cause change, and identify the one which changes most frequently. Sampling must occur at least as often as the most frequently changing factor in the process. For example, if a process has exhibited the behavior shown in the diagram below, how often should sampling occur in order to get an accurate picture of the process?

If sampling were done only at the times represented by the peaks of the curve, one would not get an accurate picture of the process, causing potentially incorrect decisions to be made. A better way to sample this process would be to sample data at the times represented by the peaks, the times represented by the valleys, and probably at times between the peaks and valleys. See the figure below.

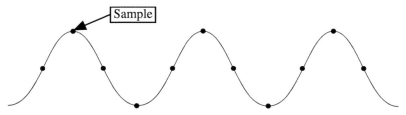

Factors to consider might be change of personnel, equipment, materials, etc. The questions which were identified in Step 1 may give guidance to this step.

Common frequencies of sampling are hourly, daily, weekly, or monthly. Although frequency is usually stated in time, it can also be stated in number: every tenth patient, every fifth pharmacy order, every other clinical record, every tenth medical bill, for example.

In example one, the STAT lab turnaround time was not expected to change often. The team decided to repeat the data collection in 2 months after changes were developed.

In example two, the team was interested in studying the variability from day to day. The 8 AM sampling time was chosen because the discharge report would be available for the previous day. So the sampling frequency was daily at that time.

3. DETERMINE THE ACTUAL FREQUENCY TIMES.

The purpose of this step is to state the actual time to take the samples. For instance, if the frequency were determined to be daily, what time of day should the sample be taken—in the morning at 8:00, around midday, or late in the day around 5:00? The actual time should be chosen as close to any expected changes in the process as possible. If the frequency were chosen to be monthly, what day of the month and what time of the day should the sample be taken?

In the first example, the team decided to do its data collection each day of the week at 8 a.m., noon, 4 p.m., 8 p.m., and 12 midnight because these are peak times for STAT demand.

In the second example, the team chose to take the daily sample starting at 8 a.m. each day, Monday through Friday, because that was when the patient disposition report from the previous day (as of midnight) was published.

Record the information from Steps 2 and 3 under the column marked "how often" on the data gathering form.

4. SELECT THE SUBGROUP (SAMPLE) SIZE.

The subgroup size is denoted by the small letter "n." You will often hear the terms "subgroup" and "sample" used interchangeably. Choosing the subgroup size is different for variables data and attributes data. Remember, variables data is that which is measured, such as height, weight, time, length, or dollars. The most common measure in health care is time: e.g., time between appointments, time to admit, time to treat, time to return to work, waiting or transfer time, time between safety incidents, time between repeat C-Sections. Attributes data on the other hand, is that which is counted, such as number of patients, number of errors per medical bill, number of missed appointments, or number of complaints.

In the examples, "number of discrepancies per medical bill" is attributes data, and the "average STAT lab turnaround time" is variables data. For variables data, go to step a, and for attributes data, go to Step b.

a. Select the subgroup size if measuring variables data.

A subgroup (or sample) is the number of items chosen to be examined at the same time. When measuring variables data, a subgroup size larger than one is preferable because larger subgroups sizes yield greater possibilities for analysis. But sometimes it is not possible to get a subgroup size larger than one. Some examples of data which may be recorded in a subgroup of one in a hospital are: cost per member per month, average monthly LOS, or average ICU bed days/month. In situations such as these when a subgroup size larger than one does not make sense, the subgroup (or sample) size is equal to one.

If a subgroup size larger than one can be chosen, then the size is usually between three and eight. A subgroup size between three and eight has been determined to be statistically efficient. The most commonly-used subgroup size is five. When more data is desired, the frequency of taking samples, not the subgroup size, should be increased.

The first example demonstrates how to gather data on processing time, which is variables data. The team decided to choose the subgroup size of five. So they will be taking 5 STAT turnaround times in a row each day at 8 a.m., 12 noon, 4 p.m., 8 p.m., and 12 midnight, and recording the average times per week at each hospital.

Enter the subgroup size, five in this case, under the column marked "how much" on the data gathering form.

b. Select the subgroup size if counting attributes data.

A subgroup (or sample) is the number of items selected to be examined at the same time. The subgroup size for attributes data depends on the process you are sampling. The general rule of thumb is to gather a large enough sample each time so that all possible characteristics you are looking for will show up.

Enter the subgroup size—5 medical bills per day for each of 3 clerks in this case—under the column marked "how much" on the data gathering form.

 REMEMBER

1. Sampling guides the quantitative study of a system.

2. Sampling is used to reduce cost and improve statistical accuracy.

3. Sample frequency depends on how fast a process changes.

 OTHER HEALTH CARE EXAMPLES

- Length of stay in subgroups of 5 consecutive cases for each of 4 different physicians

- Cost per case for a particular DRG in subgroups of 3 consecutive cases for each of 3 different group practices

- Waiting times in subgroups of 5 consecutive patients at 8 a.m., 2 p.m., and 4 p.m. in each of 3 clinics

- Number of complications per 10 consecutive surgeries of a particular type

SCATTER DIAGRAM

SCATTER DIAGRAM

 ## WHAT IS IT?

A scatter diagram helps to evaluate the relationship between two factors. It is a graph showing the plotted values of the two factors: each point on the graph represents a pair of measures. One factor is plotted on the horizontal axis and the other on the vertical. The purpose of the scatter diagram is to identify whether the two factors are related. The pattern formed by the plotted values indicates whether a relationship exists. If a relationship does exist, we say the factors are correlated.

We use scatter diagrams to analyze causes. Scatter diagrams provide a way to test hunches. For instance, consider a patient education team trying to improve diabetic education attendance. Each seminar is fully booked with 20 attendees, but not all scheduled actually attend. The team may do a scatter diagram comparing the number of people who attend each seminar with the corresponding number of days between that session's "seminar reminder" notification to attendees and the seminar date. They may find that the earlier they send seminar reminders, the higher the number of attendees.

The scatter diagram does not prove a cause-and-effect relationship exists. It does, however, verify a relationship exists and indicates that using that relationship to improve the system is likely to be effective. A cause-and-effect relationship will be verified only when the improvement is tested and the results are studied using a control chart. On the other hand, the patient education team may find there is little or no relationship—it makes little or no difference in attendance if reminder notices are sent out early. The team should then investigate other factors until a relationship is found.

~ᴏᴏ WHAT DOES IT LOOK LIKE?

A completed scatter diagram made by a team trying to reduce the number of late medications in a hospital is shown below. The team suspected that the number of medication orders being phoned in from the inpatient units was causing a delay in inpatient medication delivery.

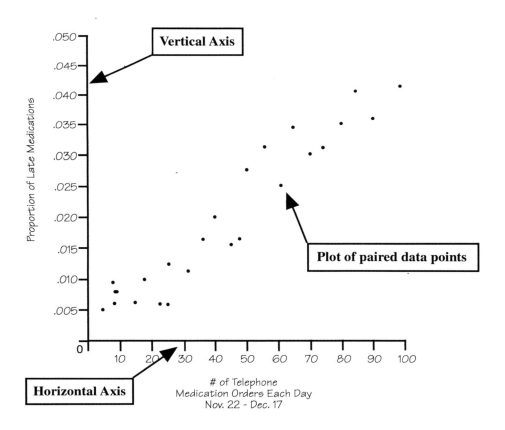

WHEN IS IT USED?

Use a scatter diagram when you can answer "yes" to both these questions:

1. **Do you want to test whether the performance of one factor is related to the performance of another?** You may suspect a relationship exists, but you will not know for sure unless you collect and analyze data.

2. **Are the two factors:**

   a) a quality characteristic (system performance measure) and a factor you suspect affects it, OR

   b) two related quality characteristics (system performance measures), OR

   c) two factors suspected of relating to the same quality characteristic (system performance measure)?

HOW IS IT MADE?

These steps assume that a check sheet containing paired observations of the two factors being studied has already been completed. A minimum of 25 pairs of data is desirable. The check sheet with the 25 pairs of data for the example is shown below. The first number in each pair is the number of telephone medication orders on a given day. The second number in each pair is the proportion of late medications for that same day.

Data for Scatter Diagram	
(# of phone requests that day, proportion of late medications that day)	
(15, .005)	(17, .006)
(43, .016)	(46, .017)
(10, .007)	(50, .029)
(18, .008)	(60, .027)
(63, .036)	(10, .007)
(14, .006)	(23, .005)
(19, .008)	(75, .030)
(70, .028)	(55, .031)
(24, .005)	(27, .013)
(80, .035)	(85, .043)
(32, .011)	(90, .036)
(35, .015)	(100, .042)
(40, .018)	

1. DRAW AND LABEL THE HORIZONTAL AND VERTICAL AXES.

Draw the horizontal and vertical axes to the lengths you wish the final scatter diagram to be. Make both about the same length.

Label each axis with the factor names and the measurement unit. It is customary to place what is believed to be the influencing factor on the x-axis (horizontal). The vertical axis is labeled with the name of the factor that is believed to respond to changes in the other factor. (The influencing factor is sometimes called the independent factor and the responding factor the dependent. However, a scatter diagram cannot prove cause-and-effect relationships.) Also, add the date to the diagram.

In this example, the measurement unit is proportion of late medications, so label the vertical axis as such. The causal factor is believed to be the number of telephone medication orders. The horizontal axis is labeled with "number of telephone medication orders." The example completed through this step is shown below.

Proportion of Late Medications

# of Telephone Medication Orders
Nov 22-Dec 17

2. SCALE EACH AXIS.

Divide the length of the axis you have drawn into enough segments to accommodate the range of values from the check sheet. Divide the axes to make room for the largest possible picture of the data. It is important that the same proportion of each axis is used. In other words, do not use only half the vertical axis and all the horizontal. Instead, use the entire vertical and the entire horizontal. From the example, the values to be plotted on the horizontal axis (number of telephone medication orders range from 10-100. Thus, a logical scaling for the horizontal axis would be ten divisions of ten each, to accommodate a value as high as 100.

The values to be plotted on the vertical axis (proportion of late medications daily) range from .005 to .043. To accommodate these values, scale the vertical axis with ten divisions of .005 each. The width of the categories for both axes should be approximately equal, if possible, to avoid incorrect results due to scaling errors. The example completed through this step is shown below.

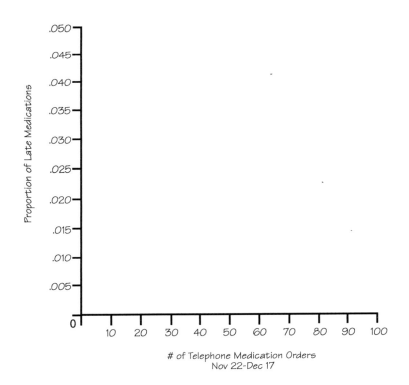

# of Telephone Medication Orders
Nov 22-Dec 17

180

3. PLOT THE POINTS.

Plot a single point on the graph for each observed pair from the data sheet. The suspected causal factor should be the value for the horizontal axis. The suspected resulting factor should be the value for the vertical axis. Count out to the right, then up for each pair, and make a dot. In the example, the first paired observation is (15, .005). In other words, on this day there were 15 telephone medication orders and .005 of all the medications filled were late.

To plot this point, count over to the point on the horizontal axis that represents 5 and from there count up to the point corresponding to .005 on the vertical axis. Make a dot at this intersection.

The second paired observation is (43, .016). Thus, count over to 43 on the horizontal axis and up to .016 and make a dot. The example with the first two paired observations plotted is shown below.

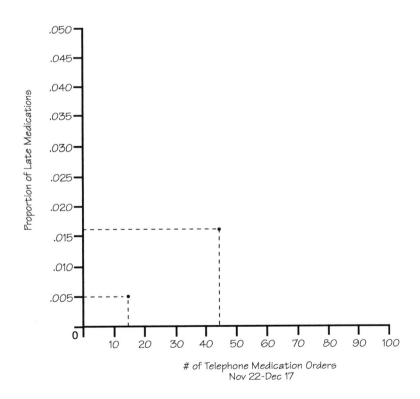

© PQ Systems, Inc.
Health Care

181

Continue plotting until all pairs of data have been plotted. The completed example is shown below.

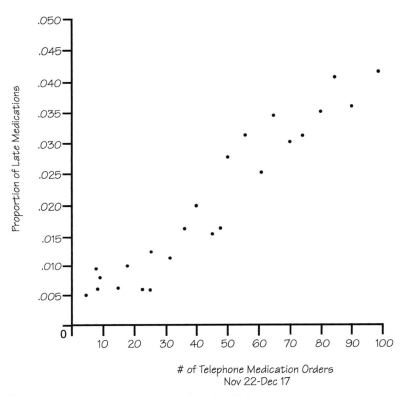

# of Telephone Medication Orders
Nov 22-Dec 17

4. INTERPRET THE SCATTER DIAGRAM.

a. **Look for patterns in the plot.**

1. A **narrow band of points** extending from the lower left to the upper right suggests a positive correlation. Positive correlation means that as one factor increases, so does the other. A narrow band extending from upper left to lower right suggests a negative correlation. Negative correlation means that the factors react opposite to one another: As one increases, the other decreases. When either of these conditions is present, it is possible to predict the approximate value of one factor when you know the value of the other.

2. A **circular pattern** suggests that no correlation or relationship exists between the two factors you are studying. There is no way to predict reliably one factor from the other. (See "Getting the most from scatter diagrams" for suggestions about how to continue with further analysis of the data that forms this pattern.)

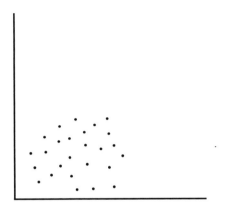

3. **Peaks or troughs** in the band of data points suggest that the relationship between the factors changes direction over the range of values studied. Consider, for example the relationship between the number of minutes of explanation about their medical condition provided to an outpatient and the patient satisfaction score. As the number of minutes rises, patient satisfaction scores may rise quickly. If too much time is taken, however, we may see patient satisfaction scores drop rapidly. The peak formed by the data on the scatter diagram reflects this growth pattern.

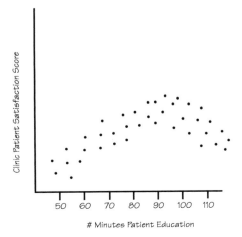

b. **Look for outliers in the plot.**

Outliers are points that do not fall into the pattern of the others. They do not cluster with the other points. If you find such points, you should investigate why they appear. The most likely cause is a measurement error. It is possible, however, that a point that looks like an outlier may be a signal of a process change or even a change in the relationship between the factors.

Looking at the completed example, it is apparent that a relationship exists between the number of telephone medication orders per day and the proportion of late medications. The dots form a band that moves in an upward direction to the right. Thus, the relationship is said to be positive. It is difficult to know to what degree, if any, that telephone medication orders contributed to the proportion of late medications. Remember, the scatter diagram does not prove cause-and-effect relationships.

However, results of the scatter diagram should raise a red flag where the number of telephone medication orders is high. The team can direct its efforts toward limiting the interruptions caused by telephone orders. And in fact, the group installed an answering machine to handle all telephone medication orders and a process to retrieve and fill these orders in an appropriate time frame without disruption to the rest of the medication delivery process. The action resulted in a significant drop in the proportion of late medications, as shown on the control chart. Only the control chart can verify that the relationship exists. The scatter diagram simply indicates the two factors are related.

REMEMBER

1. A scatter diagram can be constructed if a relationship is thought to exist between two system factors.

2. A scatter diagram is used to analyze causes.

3. The pattern, if any, formed by the points of the scatter diagram gives information about how the factors are related.

GETTING THE MOST FROM SCATTER DIAGRAMS

To use scatter diagrams most effectively, one needs to be aware of the possibility of changing patterns in the relationship between the two factors. A regression analysis (further statistical study of the data) or stratification of the data may be needed.

Caution is required when interpreting a scatter diagram. The results may be misleading when there is a third intervening factor. Consider this study conducted in a blood bank. The objective was to reduce the wait time for donors at the blood bank. They first made a scatter diagram comparing "wait time" with "number of phlebotomists." As Figure 1 below suggests, the diagram shows that wait time increases as the number of phlebotomists increases.

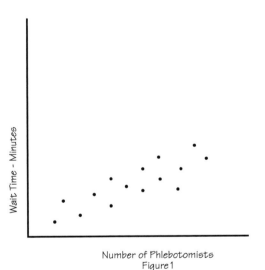

Number of Phlebotomists
Figure 1

In this case a misguided solution would be to hire fewer phlebotomists in order to reduce wait time. From our own experience, we know that reducing the number of phlebotomists would only increase wait time. What they failed to realize is that there is a relationship between the number of donors and the number of phlebotomists needed (see Figure 2 on the following page).

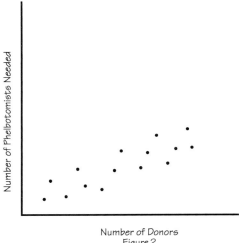

Number of Donors
Figure 2

What this second diagram fails to do is to tell the team anything about wait time, which is what they want to reduce. A third diagram below, shows the relationship between the number of donors and wait time. As the number of donors increases so does the wait time. However, this third diagram will not help the team plan to reduce wait time. Obviously, they do not want to reduce the number of donors!

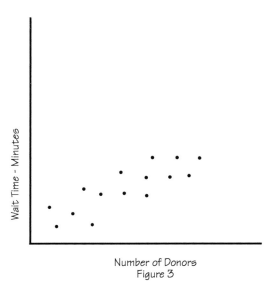

Number of Donors
Figure 3

The first three diagrams show that there is an interaction among the three factors: wait time, the number of donors, and the number of phlebotomists.

The solution to this interaction is to make the scatter diagram as follows:

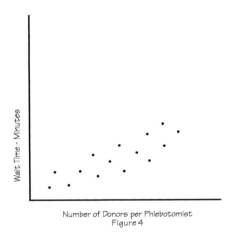

Number of Donors per Phlebotomist
Figure 4

This fourth diagram leads the team to the correct solution: Reduce the number of donors per phlebotomist. In this case, to improve the system they utilized adjacent clinic nursing staff to help during peak hours.

Although this example and its solution are obvious to anyone who has ever been in a crowded blood bank, in practice the situation may not be so clear. Always study your problem carefully to be sure you have not included an intervening factor that leads you to false conclusions.

As previously noted in the interpretation step, the relationship between two factors can change directions during the range of values being studied. When making a scatter diagram, plan to plot data over a long enough range of time for such a change of direction to appear, before drawing conclusions. If you do not plan broadly enough, you may wrongly assume that the relationship continues in one direction. For example, consider the earlier comparison between the number of minutes of patient education provided and the patient satisfaction score. The more time is spent providing information to the patient the greater satisfaction is enhanced—up to a certain point (see the figure on the following page). After this turning point, patient satisfaction scores begin to decrease. If the relationship between time taken to provide patient education and patient satisfaction scores is not tested over a long enough period of time, it may appear that more is always better! Unfortunately, there is not a hard-and-fast rule for choosing the right interval for testing. In general, it is risky to generalize that a relationship exists beyond the limits of the data gathered.

Scatter Diagram

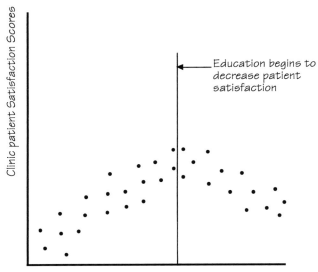

Clinic patient Satisfaction Scores

Regression analysis is a statistical technique for producing an equation to describe a line that most nearly fits the data on a scatter diagram. Given the equation, values of one factor can be substituted to predict what the other might be. The equation can also be used to draw the line on the scatter diagram. Regression analysis produces a number called a correlation coefficient which helps to describe the strength of the relationship between the two factors being studied. For any scatter diagram, the correlation coefficient (whose symbol is r) falls between positive and negative 1. Symbolically, we would say $-1 < r < +1$. If there is an exact relationship from one factor to the other, the correlation is said to be perfect and $r = 1$ (either positive or negative, depending on the relationship). If there is no relationship from one factor to the other, there is said to be no correlation and $r = 0$. Obviously, the closer r is to positive or negative 1, the stronger the correlation or relationship between the factors. Weaker correlations approach zero. To make the calculations for regression analysis, follow the directions and formula in any standard statistics book. Computer programs often make these calculations, and some hand-held calculators will also do them.

What is important to know about regression analysis is that a scatter diagram should be done first. The same regression line could be drawn from completely different point distributions. Look at the four scatter diagrams, taken from Hitoshi Kume's *Statistical Methods for Quality Improvement*, on the following page. The first figure looks as if the line fits the point distribution perfectly. But Figure 2 shows a curved point distribution so a straight line would not be appropriate. Figure 3 shows an

188

outlier (or outlying point) to be present. This point should be investigated or the measurements should be repeated. Figure 4 shows only two values, 8 and 19. Point 19 has a great influence on the regression line. In this case it would be best to gather more data.

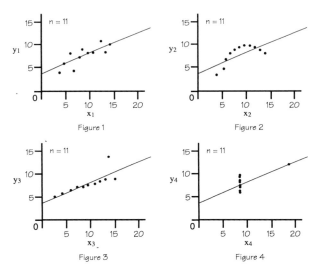

Sometimes the scatter diagram forms a circular-looking pattern that looks as if there is no correlation. When this pattern appears, it is a good idea to check the data for stratification. Perhaps the data was collected from three locations, from two time periods, or some other grouping. Data which does not reveal correlations when pooled or lumped together may show a relationship when split apart by groupings. Choose different symbols or colors with which to plot these grouping, plot all on the same graph following the steps provided above, and examine the data groups again for patterns. The figure below illustrates this idea.

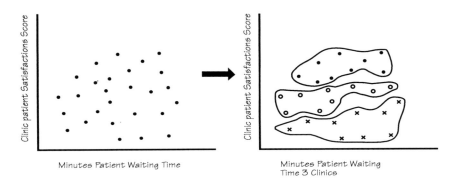

OTHER HEALTH CARE EXAMPLES

- Hours of training provided, proficiency score for that individual

- Average case load per RN, wound documentation rate per RN

- Mg/kg body weight drug given, white cell count percent change

- Patient waiting time, patient satisfaction rating

- Patient's rating of provider friendliness, patient's satisfaction rating

- Age, LOS

- Amount of pitosin given, length of labor

- Amount of drug given patient, patient's stated pain rating

VARIABLES CONTROL CHART: SUBGROUPS GREATER THAN ONE: $\overline{X}$-R CHARTS

X̄-R CONTROL CHART

🔍 WHAT IS IT?

The X̄-R chart is a picture of system data gathered over time. It shows how the mean (X̄) and range (R) of subgroups change as time goes by. These changes reflect how the system itself is changing. This chart requires data in variable or measured form.

The purpose of this control chart (or any control chart) is to minimize the chance of making two kinds of mistakes: (1) acting as though something out of the ordinary happened when nothing really did, and (2) failing to act when something out of the ordinary really happened. Statisticians call these Type I and Type II errors. One can also think of them as overcontrolling and undercontrolling.

People use X̄-R charts when they need to decide whether the system they are trying to improve is stable and predictable. That is, they use these charts to assess stability. It is only when this assessment has been made that they will know how to work on the system or what kind of improvement theory to propose.

Once an improvement theory has been implemented, we also use X̄-R charts to monitor the system to see if the theory works.

WHAT DOES IT LOOK LIKE?

A completed $\overline{X}$-R chart is shown below, indicating an individual patient measuring pm respiratory capability at home for her asthma. The principal parts of the chart are labeled for reference.

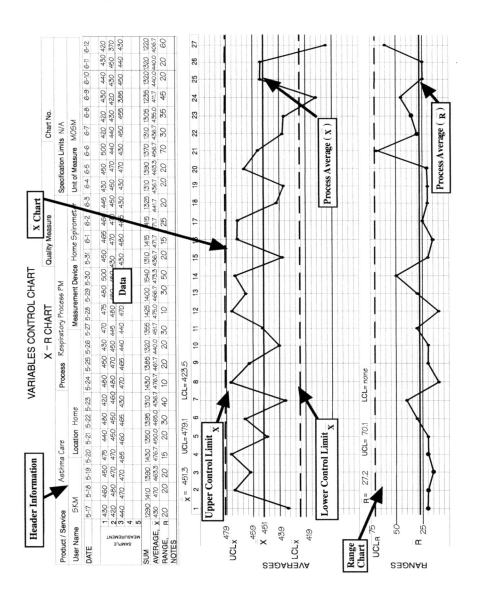

193

 WHEN IS IT USED?

Use an $\overline{X}$-R chart when you can answer "yes" to all of these questions:

1. **Do you need to assess system stability?** All control charts are used to assess stability of the system in order to minimize the chance of overcontrolling or undercontrolling the system.

2. **Is data in variables form?** Data is measurements such as time, weight, length, height, speed, or temperature normally obtained with a measuring instrument. Money is variables data because it measures value. Other charts are available for "count" or attributes data.

3. **Is data collected in subgroups larger than one?** X-MR charts are used for subgroups of one. $\overline{X}$-s charts are commonly used for subgroups of ten or more.

4. **Is the time order of subgroups preserved?** Since the control chart is designed to make it easy to study system changes over time, the order of subgroups is critical. Mixing the order of subgroups would be like developing moving film with the frames mixed. It would be like treating the patient, then doing an initial assessment, then getting their history— out of order!

HOW IS IT MADE?

These steps assume that the data has already been collected and is available. If you have already completed a run chart, all you need to do to convert it to a control chart is to select the appropriate type of control chart, calculate the grand values (Step 4), calculate the control limits (Step 5), draw the control limits and centerline (Step 7), and interpret the control chart (Step 9).

1. COMPLETE THE HEADER INFORMATION

Complete the header information at the top of the chart. Header information includes such items as product/service, user name, location, process, quality measure, measurement device, and unit of measure. It is important that this information is completed so that the chart can be read by anyone.

2. RECORD THE DATA

Record each subgroup in one column on the sheet. It is important to maintain the data in the order it was produced. Do not rearrange the order of the subgroups. All entries should have the same number of decimal places.

During data collection, record any significant changes or observations on the chart paper or on a separate process log (often located on the back of the chart paper) as these changes occur. On a chart like this one, those observations may include medication change, exercise, change in spirometer (change of equipment), illness, travel, etc.

Shown below is the example with completed header information and recorded data.

VARIABLES CONTROL CHART

X – R CHART

Product / Service	Asthma Care			Process	Respiratory Process PM				Quality Measure							Chart No.												
User Name	SKM			Location Home					Measurement Device Home Spirometer							Unit of Measure MOSM												
DATE	5-17	5-18	5-19	5-20	5-21	5-22	5-23	5-24	5-25	5-26	5-27	5-28	5-29	5-30	5-31	6-1	6-2	6-3	6-4	6-5	6-6	6-7	6-8	6-9	6-10	6-11	6-12
1	430	460	450	475	440	480	420	480	450	430	470	475	480	500	450	465	460	445	430	450	500	420	420	430	440	430	420
2	420	480	470	470	450	450	460	480	470	450	450	450	470	470	470	450	470	440	440	430	420	430	450	370
3	440	470	470	485	460	465	430	470	465	440	440	470	470	470	430	480	485	430	430	470	430	450	455	385	450	440	430
4																											
5																											
SUM																											
AVERAGE, $\overline{X}$																											
RANGE, R																											
NOTES																											

3. CALCULATE THE STATISTICS FOR EACH SUBGROUP.

a. Calculate the mean for each subgroup.

The mean $\overline{X}$, or average, is a measurement of central location. The two terms are used interchangeably in this section. The mean is the sum of the data points in the subgroup divided by the number of data points in the subgroup (n). The mean values should be recorded to at least one more decimal place than the data contains. In the example, the data goes to one decimal place, so the mean for each subgroup should go to two.

The sum of the data points in the first subgroup in this example is:

$$Sum \ X_1 = 430 + 420 + 440$$
$$= 1290$$

For this chart, the subgroup size is n = 3. Therefore, the mean for the first subgroup is:

$$\overline{X}_1 = \frac{sum \ X}{n}$$

$$= \frac{\Sigma X}{n}$$

$$= \frac{1290}{3}$$

$$= 430$$

Enter the sum and mean values for each subgroup in the corresponding rows marked "Sum" and "Average, $\overline{X}$" on the control chart paper.

b. Calculate the range for each subgroup.

The range (R) is one measurement of spread. It is the difference between the highest and the lowest data value in the subgroup. In this example, the highest value in the first subgroup is 440 and the lowest is 420. Therefore, the range is:

$$R_1 = X_{highest} - X_{lowest}$$
$$= 440 - 420$$
$$= 20$$

Enter the value for the range in the first box in the row marked "Range, R" on the control chart paper. Repeat this step for every subgroup recorded on the chart. The example completed through this step is shown below.

VARIABLES CONTROL CHART

X – R CHART		Quality Measure	Chart No.

Product / Service	Asthma Care	Process	Respiratory Process PM	Specification Limits	N/A
User Name	SKM	Location	Home	Measurement Device	Home Spirometer	Unit of Measure	MOSM

DATE	5-17	5-18	5-19	5-20	5-21	5-22	5-23	5-24	5-25	5-26	5-27	5-28	5-29	5-30	5-31	6-1	6-2	6-3	6-4	6-5	6-6	6-7	6-8	6-9	6-10	6-11	6-12
1	430	460	450	475	440	480	420	480	450	430	470	475	480	500	450	465	460	445	430	450	500	420	420	430	440	430	420
2	420	460	470	470	450	450	460	480	470	450	445	480	460	460	430	470	470	460	450	470	440	440	430	420	430	450	370
3	440	470	470	485	460	465	430	470	465	440	440	470	470	470	430	480	465	430	430	470	430	460	455	386	450	440	430
4																											
5																											
6																											
SUM	1290	1410	1390	1430	1350	1395	1310	1430	1385	1320	1355	1425	1400	1540	1310	1415	1415	1325	1310	1390	1370	1310	1305	1236	1320	1320	1220
AVERAGE, X	430	470	463.3	476.7	450.0	465.0	436.7	476.7	461.7	440.0	451.7	475.0	466.7	473.3	436.7	471.7	471.7	441.7	436.7	463.3	456.7	436.7	435.0	411.7	440.0	440.0	406.7
RANGE, R	20	20	20	15	20	30	40	10	20	20	30	10	30	50	20	15	25	20	20	20	70	30	35	45	20	20	60
NOTES																											

4. CALCULATE THE AVERAGES FOR THE SUBGROUP STATISTICS.

a. Calculate the grand mean.

The grand mean, $\overline{\overline{X}}$ (read "X double bar"), is the average of all the means calculated in the previous step. To calculate the grand mean, add the row of mean values and divide by the number of subgroups taken (known as k).

$$\overline{\overline{X}} = \frac{sum\ \overline{X}}{k}$$
$$= \frac{\sum \overline{X}}{k}$$
$$= \frac{\overline{X}_1 + \overline{X}_2 + \overline{X}_3 + \ldots + \overline{X}_k}{k}$$

In the example, $\overline{\overline{X}}$ is:

$$\overline{\overline{X}} = \frac{430 + 470 + 463 + \ldots + 406.67}{27}$$
$$= 451.3$$

The grand mean value should also contain one more decimal place than the data. Enter the value for $\overline{\overline{X}}$ in the space marked $\overline{\overline{X}}$ at the top of the chart.

© PQ Systems, Inc.
Health Care

b.   Calculate the average range.

The average range, $\overline{R}$ (read "R bar"), is the average of all the subgroup range values. It is calculated by adding the values in the range row and dividing by the number of subgroups taken (k).

$$\overline{R} = \frac{sum\ of\ ranges}{no.\ of\ subgroups}$$

$$= \frac{\Sigma\ R}{k}$$

$$= \frac{R_1 + R_2 + R_3 + ... + R_k}{k}$$

In the example $\overline{R}$ is:

$$\overline{R} = \frac{20 + 20 + 20 + ... + 60}{27}$$

$$= 27.2$$

Also, carry out the average range value one more decimal place than that of the data. Enter the value for $\overline{R}$ in the space provided at the top of the range chart.

5.   CALCULATE THE CONTROL LIMITS.

Control limits are lines drawn on the chart used as a basis for judging whether the system is statistically stable. These limits come from the variability of the system, not from the specifications set by engineering or any other source. Twenty-five to 30 subgroups provide enough data to calculate control limits. If you decide to calculate limits with fewer subgroups, think of them as "trial" limits that should be recalculated after 25 subgroups have been collected.[1]

a.   Calculate the control limits for the $\overline{X}$ chart.

The symbol for the upper control limit for the $\overline{X}$ portion of the chart is $UCL_{\overline{x}}$, and the symbol for the lower control limit is $LCL_{\overline{x}}$. The formula for the upper control limit is:

$$UCL_{\overline{X}} = \overline{\overline{X}} + (A_2 \times \overline{R})$$

A_2 is a weighting factor used in the control limit calculation. Its value is related to the size of the subgroups being taken. The value for A_2 can be found in the table that follows. The table also presents different weighting factors for various subgroup sizes. These additional factors will be used to calculate the control limits for the range chart.

---

[1]Donald J. Wheeler and David S. Chambers, *Understanding Statistical Process Control*, (Knoxville, TN: Statistical Process Controls, Inc.), p. 79.

Weighting Factors[2]

Subgroup Size (n)	A_2	D_3	D_4
2	1.880	0	3.267
3	1.023	0	2.574
4	.729	0	2.282
5	.577	0	2.114
6	.483	0	2.004
7	.419	.076	1.924
8	.373	.136	1.864
9	.337	.184	1.816

For this example with a subgroup size of 3, the value of A_2 is 1.023.

So, $UCL_{\overline{x}}$ for the example is:

$$UCL_{\overline{X}} = 451.3 + (1.023 \times 27.2)$$

$$= 479.1$$

The values for the control limits should also be carried out one more decimal place than the data values contain. The formula for the lower control limit is:

$$LCL_{\overline{X}} = \overline{\overline{X}} - \left(A_2 \times \overline{R} \right)$$

$LCL_{\overline{x}}$ for the example is:

$$LCL_{\overline{X}} = 451.3 - (1.023 \times 27.2)$$

$$= 423.4$$

If the lower control limit turns out to be a negative number and the process can have negative measurements, use the LCL. If the process measurement cannot go below zero, the negative limit has no meaning and is not used.

Write the results of the control limit calculations at the top of the chart paper in the spaces marked UCL and LCL.

---

[2] Technically, D_3 is undefined for sample sizes of six or less. For consistency in calculating the control limit, D_3 is treated as 0, making the lower control limit 0.

© PQ Systems, Inc.
Health Care

b. Calculate the control limits for the range chart.

The symbol for the upper control limit for the range is UCL_R, and the symbol for the lower control limit is LCL_R. The formula for the upper control limit for the range chart is:

$$UCL_R = D_4 \times \overline{R}$$

The value for the weighting factor, D_4, can be found in the table on the previous page. For a subgroup size of n = 3, D_4 is 2.574. So, UCL_R is:

$$UCL_R = 2.574 \text{ x } 27.2$$

$$= 70.1$$

The formula for the lower limit for the range is:

$$LCL_R = D_3 \times \overline{R}$$

The table shows the value for D_3 for a subgroup size of n = 3, or smaller, to be 0, so LCL_R is:

$$LCL_R = 0 \text{ x } 26.5$$

$$= 0$$

Write the control limits for the range chart in the spaces marked UCL and LCL at the top of the range chart.

6. DETERMINE THE SCALING FOR THE CHARTS.

Scaling means numbering the lines on the left of the chart so the points can be plotted. Scaling can be the most difficult part of constructing a control chart. When following the rules for scaling, be careful not to get caught up in trying to make the calculations perfect. The important thing is that the chart is readable and easy to make.

a. Determine the scaling for the $\overline{X}$ chart.

Begin by finding the largest $\overline{X}$ value from the data entry section of the chart. Compare this value to the upper control limit and write down the larger of the two. In this example, the largest $\overline{X}$ value is 476.67 and the upper control limit is 479.1. So write down 479.1.

Next, find and compare the smallest $\overline{X}$ value to the lower control limit, and write down the smaller of the two. In our example, 406.67 is the smallest $\overline{X}$ value and 424.2 is the lower control limit, so write 406.67.

Subtract the smaller of the two numbers from the larger, and write down the difference. Divide this difference by about two-thirds of the total number of lines on the $\overline{X}$ chart. (Use only two-thirds of the available lines in order to leave space outside the control limits to plot future shifts.)

The result of the division is the increment value for each line on the control chart.

The two values recorded are 479.1 and 406.67; their difference is 479.1 - 406.67 = 72.43. There are 30 lines on the chart paper, so use 20 lines (two-thirds) to make the chart.

$$\text{The increment value is: } \frac{72.43}{20} = 3.62$$

Round the increment value upward as necessary to get an easy number to work with, such as 1, 2, or 5. The actual value may be some multiple of ten, such as 1, 10, .1 or .01. Round 3.62 to 4.0 for the increment value of each line moving away from the grand mean. Each line stands for 4.

Place the grand mean near a line at the center of the $\overline{X}$ portion of the chart. It is not necessary that the grand mean be located exactly on the center dark reference line. If possible, position the grand mean so that you are able to label the dark center reference line with the multiple of a number such as 1, 2, 5, 10, etc.

To complete the numbering of the lines, add the line increment value to the grand mean at each small line as you move upward from the centerline. Label each main reference line (usually every fifth line) with its value.

To complete the line numbering below the grand mean, begin at the grand mean reference line and subtract the line increment value as you move downward from the center. Again, label each main reference line with its value. The example with the $\overline{X}$ portion of the chart scaled is shown below.

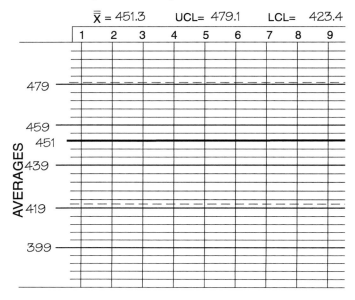

b. Determine the scaling for the range chart.

Find the largest range value in the data section of the chart. Compare it to the upper control limit and write down the larger of the two.

In this example, the largest range value is 70 and the upper control limit for the range is 70.1, so write down 70.1.

The smallest value is taken as zero in a range chart. Always begin the scale with zero at the bottom.

Subtract the smaller of the two values you wrote down from the larger, and write down the difference. The two numbers you wrote down were 70.1 and 0, so their difference is 70.1 - 0 = 70.1. To find the increment value, divide the difference (70.1) by the total number of lines on the range chart. This figure is the increment value used to scale the range chart; it should be rounded up to the same number of decimal places as the data. Again, round up to an easy digit such as a multiple of 1, 2, 5, 10, etc.

The difference is 70.1, and there are 15 lines available on the range chart.

The increment value is: $\dfrac{70.1}{15} = 4.67$

Round the increment up from 4.67 to 5.0 so the scaling will make room for the range data and will be easier to work with.

To scale the chart, label the bottom line as zero and move upward from zero, adding the line increment value as you go. Label each main reference line, usually every fifth line. The example completed through this step is shown below.

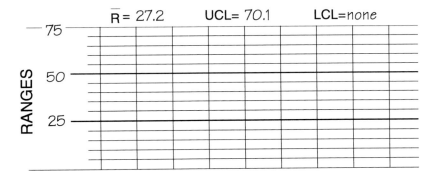

7. DRAW THE CENTERLINE AND CONTROL LIMITS

Draw a solid dark horizontal line to represent $\overline{\overline{X}}$ on the $\overline{X}$ Chart and to represent $\overline{R}$ on the range chart. Label the lines with the correct symbol, $\overline{\overline{X}}$ or $\overline{R}$. Draw a dashed horizontal line to represent each control limit (upper and lower) the $\overline{X}$ chart and the range chart. (If the LCL for the range chart has turned out to be 0, there is no need to draw a dashed line on the line that already exists for 0.) Label each control limit with the correct symbol ($\text{UCL}_{\overline{x}}$, $\text{LCL}_{\overline{x}}$, $\text{UCL}_{\overline{R}}$). The completed example is shown below.

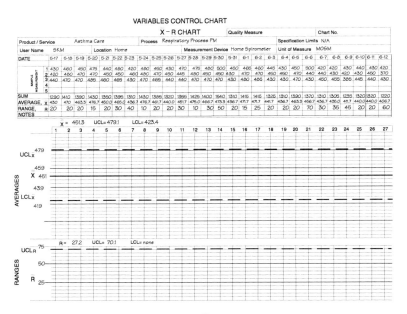

8. PLOT THE VALUES ON THE CHARTS

a. Plot the values on the $\overline{X}$ Chart.

Starting with the first subgroup, plot each subgroup's $\overline{X}$ value on the vertical line corresponding to the subgroup column on the $\overline{X}$ chart (the top chart). Connect the dots with straight lines.

b. Plot the values on the range chart.

Starting with the first subgroup, plot each range on the vertical line corresponding to the subgroup column on the range chart (the bottom chart). Connect the dots with straight lines. The example completed through this step is shown on the following page.

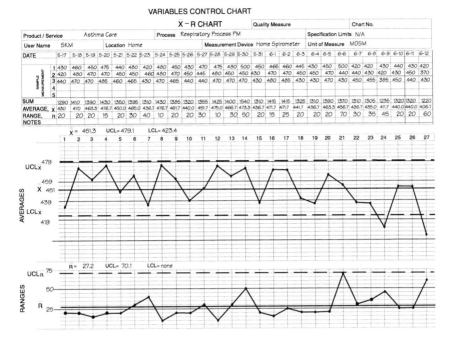

9. INTERPRET THE CONTROL CHART

Control chart interpretation uses the same basic rules for both variables and attributes control charts. Chart interpretation is explained in the "Chart Interpretation" section of these materials. However, a list of the basic rules for interpreting out-of-control conditions follows.

1. Any point lying outside the control limits

2. Run of seven points:

    a. seven or more points in a row above or below the centerline

    b. seven or more points in a row going in one direction, up or down

3. Any nonrandom pattern, including the following typical cases.

    a. too close to the average

    b. too far from the average

    c. cycles

The X̄-Bar chart in the example on the previous page shows the process to be unstable. There are two points (subgroups 24 and 27) outside the lower control limit on the X̄ chart. This out-of-control condition indicate special cause of variation in the process. In this case the patient identified the special cause to be resulting from missed medications. The patient went on an out-of-town business trip during this period, did not take her medications with her, and missed taking her medications for 4 days (subgroups 24 through 27). When the special cause has been identified, it should be written on the chart paper beside the point. The special cause which includes these 4 days was eliminated by insuring medications were resumed.

When the patient and the provider were sure the special cause had been removed, they reconstructed the control chart, deleting the subgroups showing the special cause. The new stable control chart is shown below.

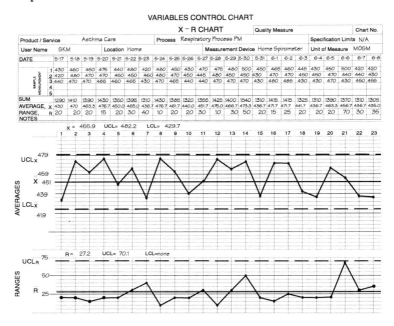

When systems are declared to be stable, the control limits calculated previously are simply drawn onto new chart paper as subgroups continue to be collected. This will allow the patient and physician to make decisions about the system's stability as each new subgroup is plotted. New control limits are calculated only when a change is made to the system (see "Getting the Most from X̄-R charts" for more discussion).

REMEMBER

1. An $\overline{X}$-R control chart shows how a system measured by variables data changes over time.

2. $\overline{X}$-R chart (like any control chart) minimizes the possibility of over- or undercontrolling the system by identifying special and common causes of system variation.

3. The subgroup size for an $\overline{X}$-R chart must be larger than one. Five is the most common subgroup size.

GETTING THE MOST FROM $\overline{X}$-R CHARTS

Getting the most from $\overline{X}$-R charts as well as other control charts means being able to use them for several different purposes as you make system improvements.

When beginning to work on system improvement, **assess stability** of the system. The purpose of assessing stability is to analyze the factors which contribute to variability. Pick an important quality characteristic of the output and track it over time with a control chart. In a manufacturing process, these characteristics are often final dimensions or difficult dimensions on the part being made. In a health care process, such a characteristic might be the overall time required to complete a task— the time to acquire a piece of medical equipment, time to fill a prescription or administer a drug, time it takes to see a patient in a clinic. One calls such measures "results data" which is a measure for baseline data. Many factors influence the overall variability of a system, but until this first chart is made, one does not know whether to work on common or special causes.

Once a system's stability has been assessed, pay special attention to the need to **stratify data**. Sometimes you will find sources of variability this way. Some clinics may cause less patient waiting time than others (see chart on following page). Or you may have a lower cost for a certain DRG than others in a system. You may find in an Emergency Department that entirely different productivity and cost results appear among shifts. You must select your subgroups and record data in a way that allows you to check for stratification by time, location, demographic, cost, DRG, and other categories.

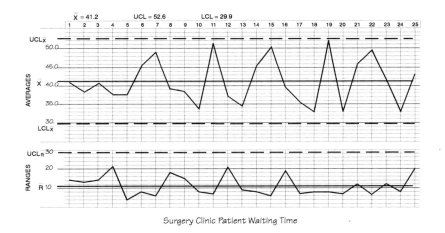

Surgery Clinic Patient Waiting Time

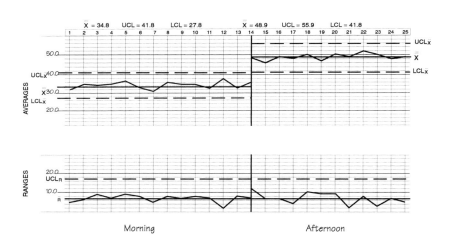

Morning   Afternoon

To **generate improvement theories,** move your investigation upstream to focus on the resources or variables that can cause variability in results/outcomes. They may be the causes identified on your cause-and-effect diagram. Often you need to apply control charts to casual variables to tell whether they are, themselves, stable. Reduce the variability in each of these factors and you will reduce the overall system variability. Suppose you discover that Health Care Facility A uses different methods and is producing consistently quicker and less expensive care for DRG 89. Standardize Health Care Facility A's methods and then replicate and test them in other areas of the system making sure you continue to track the impact of the change.

The control chart used in this way will help you to decide if the new method really makes a difference and whether the overall system is being improved.

The question of **when to calculate new control limits** always arises here. Should you calculate new limits when you standardize and replicate the Health Care Facility A's method? Yes! But wait until you see evidence that the change has had an impact on a variable, such as the system's shifting or out of control evidence. (Note: when you recalculate control limits after a system change, use only those subgroups collected after the change to recalculate control limits.) In general, once control limits have been calculated, they are simply projected onto new forms as additional data is gathered, so the operator has an ongoing way to assess stability as soon as a new subgroup is gathered and recorded. When you make a system change, you must indicate this on the chart. Then you can identify exactly which points on the chart correspond to the new method—and begin with those when you recalculate limits.

Finally, using the control chart for **standardization** means maintaining data collection throughout the process operation. Imagine that you have studied the Health Care Facility A's methods for treating DRG 89 mentioned earlier, made changes to standardize methods and stopped taking data. What would happen? First, you would have only perception and opinion to tell you whether you had made improvements by your action. More importantly, if you had shared Hospital A's methods as "best practice" but failed to measure the impact in your other hospitals, it would be difficult to know if the change was an improvement.

Using the control chart for standardization suggests that the system is well defined, that its resource variables are understood, and that its most important procedures and elements are standardized. In other words, stable, predictable systems are more likely to result when standards of operation are in place and executed routinely. Clearly, one may expect that standards and methods will change as improvements are discovered. It becomes the responsibility of the manager to communicate such changes to all concerned in order to maintain the steady streams of variability which are inevitable in even the most well-controlled processes.

✎ OTHER HEALTH CARE EXAMPLES

• Satisfaction score - subgroups of 5 customers

• Waiting times - subgroups of 3 patients

• Cost per case/subgroups of 3 for each of 5 providers

• Time to complete STAT labs in subgroups of 5

• Length of stay in subgroups of 5 cases for each of 3 physicians

VARIABLES CONTROL CHART: SUBGROUPS SIZE ONE: X-MR CHARTS

X–MR CONTROL CHART

 WHAT IS IT?

An X-MR[1] (read "individual-moving range") chart is a variables control chart for a subgroup size of one. It shows how a system changes over time by plotting individual measured values and the variability between one data point and the next. The X-MR chart is used when a subgroup size larger than one is not practical or desirable. Examples of use for X-MR chart in health care are: cost per member per month for HMO or Home Health Agencies; monthly patient satisfaction ratings, dollars in accounts receivable per week, supply costs per day or week or month, cost per hip replacement, days between repeat c-sections, days between falls, medication errors, or any other undesirable event.

The purpose of this control chart (or any control chart) is to minimize the chance of making one of two kinds of mistakes: (1) acting as though something out of the ordinary happened when nothing really did, and (2) failing to act when something out of the ordinary really happened. Statisticians call these Type I and Type II errors. We can also think of them as overcontrolling and undercontrolling.

People use X-MR charts to decide whether the system they are trying to improve is stable and predictable. That is, they use it to assess stability. Only then will they know what kind of improvement theory to propose. Once the improvement theory is implemented, we use the chart to monitor the system to see if the theory works. We may also use an X-MR chart to stratify data.

---

[1] This is the symbolic notation used for this chart. You will often see it in references by its longer name. This chart is also referred to as an "individuals chart."

∽◯◯ WHAT DOES IT LOOK LIKE?

A completed example of an X-MR control chart is shown below. A group used this chart to assess stability and monitor vent time over time. The main parts are labeled for reference.

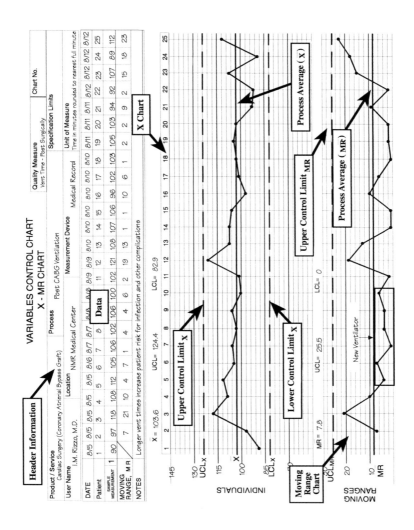

⟲ WHEN IS IT USED?

Use an X-MR control chart when you can answer "yes" to all these questions:

1. **Do you need to assess system stability?** All control charts are used to assess stability of the system in order to minimize the chance of overcontrolling or undercontrolling the system.

2. **Is the data in variables form?** Variables data is measurements such as height, weight, length, pressure, time, money, temperature. Increasingly, "through put" data such as number of patient visits per week, surgeries per week, consults per month, phone calls per day, etc. is being treated as variables data in health care and charted using an X-MR chart. Other control charts are available for attributes or "count" data.

3. **Is the data collected in subgroups of one?** This means single data points, not groups. $\overline{X}$-R, $\tilde{X}$-R, and $\overline{X}$-s charts are used to chart variables data with subgroups larger than one.

4. **Is the time order of subgroups preserved?** Since the control chart is designed to make it easy to study system changes over time, the order of subgroups is critical. Mixing the order of subgroups would be like developing moving film with the frames mixed. It would be like treating the patient, then doing an initial assessment, then getting their history—out of order!

 How is it made?

These steps assume the data has been previously collected and recorded on a data collection sheet or on control chart paper. One data point will be recorded for each subgroup. Like all control charts, however, a run chart will probably exist. If so, simply calculate the moving ranges (Step 3), calculate the overall averages (Step 4), calculate control limits (Step 5), draw the centerline and control limits (Step 7), and interpret the chart (Step 9).

1. COMPLETE THE HEADER INFORMATION.

Complete the header information on the chart. The header information includes such items as product/service, user name, process, location, and quality measure. It is always important to complete this information so that others can understand the chart.

2. RECORD THE DATA.

If the data was not recorded on the chart paper as it was collected, record the collected data in the appropriate area on the chart. Record one data point for each subgroup in the row marked "Sample Measurement" on the chart paper. The example with completed header information and recorded data is shown below.

VARIABLES CONTROL CHART
X - MR CHART

Quality Measure	Chart No.
Vent Time - Post Surgically	

Product / Service					Process								Specification Limits								
Cardiac Surgery (Coronary Atrierial Bypass Graft)					Post CABG Ventilation																

User Name			Location				Measurement Device					Unit of Measure									
I.M. Rizzo, M.D.			NMR Medical Center				Medical Record					Time in minutes rounded to nearest full minute									

DATE		8/5	8/5	8/5	8/5	8/5	8/6	8/7	8/7	8/8	8/8	8/9	8/9	8/10	8/10	8/10	8/10	8/10	8/10	8/11	8/11	8/11	8/12	8/12	8/12	8/12
TIME		1	2	3	4	5	6	7	8	9	10	11	12	13	14	15	16	17	18	19	20	21	22	23	24	25
SAMPLE MEASUREMENT 1		90	97	118	108	112	105	106	102	106	100	102	121	108	107	106	96	102	103	105	103	94	92	107	89	112
MOVING RANGE, M R																										
NOTES																										

3. CALCULATE THE MOVING RANGES.

The moving range is the difference between consecutive readings, ignoring negative signs. Technically, the moving range is the absolute value of the difference between one data point and the next. (The symbol for absolute value is two vertical bars, one at each end of the expression.) The absolute value is used so there will be no negative moving ranges.

The first moving range is the absolute value of the second subgroup minus the value of the first subgroup. The first moving range is entered under the second subgroup reading in the row marked "Moving Range, MR" on the chart paper. No moving range value exists under the first reading, because it would have no meaning. (Notice that the first box has a slash through it to remind you not to use it.) Note: there will be one less moving range than the number of subgroups.

$$MR_1 = |X_2 - X_1|$$
$$= |97 - 90|$$
$$= |7|$$
$$= 7$$

The second moving range is the absolute value of the third subgroup minus the value of the second subgroup. The value for the second moving range is entered under the third subgroup reading.

$$MR_2 = |X_3 - X_2|$$
$$= |118 - 97|$$
$$= |21|$$
$$= 21$$

The example with the first few moving ranges entered is shown below.

VARIABLES CONTROL CHART
X - MR CHART

Product / Service					Process								
Cardiac Surgery (Coronary Atrierial Bypass Graft)					Post CABG Ventilation								

User Name				Location					Measurement Device				
I.M. Rizzo, M.D.				NMR Medical Center									

DATE	8/5	8/5	8/5	8/5	8/5	8/6	8/7	8/7	8/8	8/8	8/9	8/9	8/10	8/10
TIME	1	2	3	4	5	6	7	8	9	10	11	12	13	14
SAMPLE MEASUREMENT 1	90	97	118	108	112	105	106	102	106	100	102	121	108	107	1(
MOVING RANGE, M R		7	21	10	4	7	1	4	4	6	2	19	13	1
NOTES														

X =   UCL=   LCL=

1   2   3   4   5   6   7   8   9   10   11   1~

Continue calculating the moving range for each pair of subgroups. The example completed through this step is shown below.

VARIABLES CONTROL CHART
X - MR CHART

Quality Measure	Chart No.
Vent Time- Post Surgically	

Product / Service					Process									Specification Limits										
Cardiac Surgery (Coronary Atrierial Bypass Graft)								Post CABG Ventilation																

User Name					Location						Measurement Device					Unit of Measure								
I.M. Rizzo, M.D.					NMR Medical Center							Medical Record				Time in minutes rounded to nearest full minute								

DATE	8/5	8/5	8/5	8/5	8/5	8/6	8/7	8/7	8/8	8/8	8/9	8/9	8/10	8/10	8/10	8/10	8/10	8/10	8/11	8/11	8/11	8/12	8/12	8/12	8/12
TIME	1	2	3	4	5	6	7	8	9	10	11	12	13	14	15	16	17	18	19	20	21	22	23	24	25
SAMPLE MEASUREMENT 1	90	97	118	108	112	105	106	102	106	100	102	121	108	107	106	96	102	103	105	103	94	92	107	89	112
MOVING RANGE, M R		7	21	10	4	7	1	4	4	6	2	19	13	1	1	10	6	1	2	2	9	2	15	18	23
NOTES																									

4. CALCULATE THE OVERALL AVERAGES.

a. Calculate the average for the individual chart.

The average ($\overline{X}$) is an average of all the data points recorded. It is found by adding the data points and dividing by the number of subgroups taken (k).

$$\overline{X} = \frac{sum \ of \ data \ points}{no. \ of \ subgroups}$$

$$= \frac{\Sigma X}{k}$$

$$= \frac{X_1 + X_2 + X_3 + \ldots + X_k}{k}$$

In the example $\overline{X}$ is:

$$\overline{X} = \frac{90 + 97 + 118 + \ldots + 112}{25}$$

$$= \frac{2,591}{25}$$

$$= 103.6$$

The value for $\overline{X}$ should be recorded with one more decimal place than the data. The data for the chart in the example has no decimal values so $\overline{X}$ should go to one decimal place. Record the value for $\overline{X}$ on the chart at the top of the paper in the space provided.

b. Calculate the average moving range.

Calculate $\overline{MR}$, the average moving range.[2] The average moving range is found by adding all the values in the moving range row and dividing by the number of moving ranges. This is the number of subgroups taken minus one (k-1). Remember, there is no moving range value entered under subgroup one. The example chart has 25 subgroups so k - 1 = 24.

$$\overline{MR} = \frac{MR_1 + MR_2 + MR_3 + \dots + MR_{k-1}}{k-1}$$

$$= \frac{7 + 21 + 10 + \dots + 23}{24}$$

$$= \frac{188}{24}$$

$$= 7.8$$

$\overline{MR}$ is also recorded with one decimal place more than the data contains. Enter the value found for $\overline{MR}$ at the top of the moving range chart in the space provided.

5. CALCULATE THE CONTROL LIMITS.

In order to assess the stability of the system, you must calculate the control limits. Control limits are lines drawn on the control chart used as a basis for judging whether or not the system is stable. These limits come from the variability of the system—not from the specifications, targets, or benchmarks set by payers, or any other source. Twenty-five to thirty subgroups provide enough data to calculate control limits. If you decide to calculate limits with fewer subgroups, think of them as "trial" limits that should be recalculated after 25 subgroups have been collected.[3]

a. Calculate the control limits for the individual chart.

The formula for the upper control limit for the individual chart (UCL_x) is:

$$UCL_X = \overline{X} + (E_2 \times \overline{MR})$$

---

[2] Western Electric, *Statistical Quality Control Handbook* (Indianapolis, IN: AT&T Technologies, 1985 printing). The average moving range is also denoted in other references as R.

[3] Donald J. Wheeler and David S. Chambers, *Understanding Statistical Process Control* (Knoxville, TN: Statistical Process Control, Inc., 1986), p. 79.

A list of weighting factors used to construct this chart is shown at the end of this step. For a subgroup size of 2, $E_2 = 2.660$. We use the E_2 value for a subgroup size of n = 2 because two subgroups are used in determining the moving range.

UCL_x for the example is:

$$UCL_X = 103.6 + (2.660 \times 7.8)$$

$$= 103.6 + 20.75$$

$$= 124.4$$

The formula for the lower control limit for the individual chart (LCL_x) is:

$$LCL_x = \bar{X} - (E_2 \times M\bar{R})$$

LCL_x for the example is:

$$LCL_x = 103.6 - (2.660 \times 7.8)$$

$$= 103.6 - 20.75$$

$$= 82.9$$

The control limit values are also recorded with one more decimal place than the data. Write the values for both control limits in the space provided at the top of the individual chart.

b. Calculate the control limits for the moving range chart.

The formula for the upper control limit for the moving range chart (UCL_{MR}) is:

$$UCL_{MR} = D_4 \times M\bar{R}$$

The value for D_4 for a subgroup size of 2 is 3.267.

UCL_{MR} for the example is:

$$UCL_{MR} = 3.267 \times 7.8$$

$$= 25.5$$

The formula for the lower control limit for the moving range chart (LCL_{MR}) is:

$$LCL_{MR} = D_3 \times M\bar{R}$$

For a subgroup size of n = 2, the value for D_3 is 0, so (LCL_{MR}) is:

$$LCL_{MR} = 0 \times 7.8$$
$$= 0$$

Write the values for the control limits for the moving range at the top of the moving range chart in the space provided.

Weighting Factors

Subgroup Size (n)	E_2	D_3	D_4
2	2.660	0	3.267

Remember, we use n = 2 when choosing weighting factors because the calculation of the control limits is based on the fact that two subgroups are used to find the moving range.

6. DETERMINE THE SCALING FOR THE CHARTS.

Scaling means numbering the lines on the left of the chart so the points can be plotted. Scaling can be the most difficult and inexact part of constructing a control chart. When following the steps for scaling, be careful not to get caught up in trying to make the calculations perfect. What is important is that the chart is readable and easy to make.

a. Determine the scaling for the individual chart.

Begin by finding the largest individual value from the data entry section on the chart. Compare this value to the upper control limit and write down the larger of the two. In this example, the largest individual value is 121 and the upper control limit is 124.4, so write down 124.4.

Next, find and compare the smallest individual value to the lower control limit and write down the smaller of the two. In the example, 89 is the smallest individual value and 82.9 is the lower control limit, so write down 82.9.

Subtract the smaller of the two values you wrote down from the larger and keep the difference. Divide this difference by about two-thirds of the total number of lines on the individual chart. Use only two-thirds of the available lines in order to leave space outside the control limits to plot shifts in the future. The result of the division is the increment value for each line on the control chart.

The two values written down are 124.4 and 82.9, so their difference is 124.4 - 82.9 = 41.5. There are 30 lines on the chart paper, so use 20 lines (two-thirds) to find the increment value.

The increment value is: $\dfrac{41.5}{20} = 2.1$

The increment value should be rounded upward as necessary so the dark reference lines (usually every fifth line) can be labeled with an easy-to-work-with number such as a multiple of 1, 2, 5, 10. Round 2.1 to 3 for the increment value of each line moving away from the center of the chart.

Place the average ($\overline{X}$) on or close to a line at the center of the individual chart. For instance, in the example the value for $\overline{X}$ is 103.6. Locate $\overline{X}$ a little more than one line above the center dark reference line. Label the center dark reference line 100. To complete the numbering of the lines, add the increment value (3) to the center dark reference line (labeled 100) as you move upward. As you are moving upward, label the dark reference lines. In the example, the dark reference lines above 100 are labeled 115, 130, and 145.

To complete the line numbering below the average, begin at the line nearest to $\overline{X}$ (100 in this case) and subtract the line increment value (3) as you move downward from the center. Again, label each dark reference line. In the example, the dark reference lines below 100 are labeled 85, 70, and 55. The example individual chart with scaling complete is shown below.

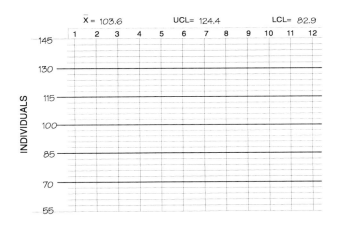

b. Determine the scaling for the moving range chart.

Find the largest moving range value in the data section of the chart. Compare it to the upper control limit and write down the larger of the two.

In this example, the largest moving range value is 23 and the upper control limit for the moving range is 25.5, so we write down 25.5.

The smallest value is taken as zero as in a moving range chart. We always begin the scale with zero at the bottom.

To find the increment value, subtract the two numbers you wrote down (25.5 and 0) and divide the difference by the total number of lines on the range chart. This figure is the increment value used to scale the moving range chart.

The two numbers written down are 25.5 and 0, so their difference is 25.5 - 0 = 25.5. Fifteen lines are available on the moving range chart, so the increment value is:

$$\frac{25.5}{15} = 1.7$$

Round the increment value to 2 so the scaling will make room for the moving ranges. Remember, when rounding for scaling you should always round up.

To scale the chart, label the bottom line as zero and move upward from zero, adding the line increment as you go. Label each dark reference line. In the example, label the dark reference lines 0, 10, 20, 30. The example completed through this step is shown below.

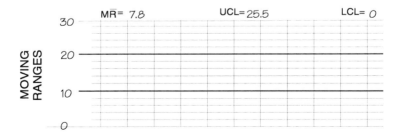

7. DRAW THE CENTERLINES AND CONTROL LIMITS.

Draw dark horizontal centerlines on each chart representing $\overline{X}$ and $\overline{MR}$. Draw dashed horizontal lines on each chart representing the control limits. Label the lines with the appropriate label e.g., UCL_X, LCL_X, UCL_{MR}, LCL_{MR}, $\overline{X}$, and $\overline{MR}$. The example completed through this step is shown below.

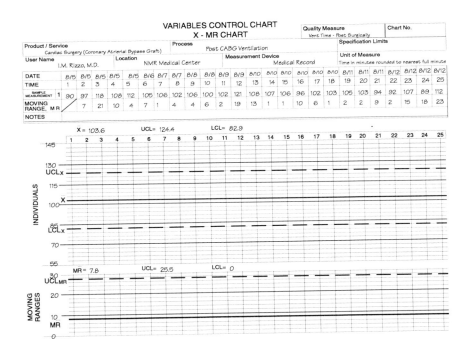

8. PLOT THE VALUES ON THE CHARTS.

Plot each data point on the corresponding vertical line on the individual chart. Plot each moving range value on the moving range chart. Remember, the moving range chart will have one fewer plot than on the individual chart (subgroup 1 has no moving range value). Connect the dots with straight lines. The example completed through this step is shown below.

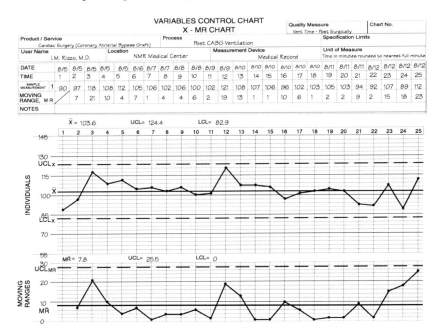

VARIABLES CONTROL CHART
X - MR CHART

Quality Measure														Chart No.											

Quality Measure: Vent Time - Post Surgically

Product / Service Cardiac Surgery (Coronary Arterial Bypass Graft)
Process Post CABG Ventilation
Specification Limits

User Name I.M. Rizzo, M.D.
Location NMR Medical Center
Measurement Device Medical Record
Unit of Measure Time in minutes rounded to nearest full minute

DATE	8/5	8/5	8/5	8/5	8/5	8/6	8/7	8/7	8/8	8/8	8/9	8/9	8/10	8/10	8/10	8/10	8/10	8/10	8/11	8/11	8/11	8/12	8/12	8/12	8/12
TIME	1	2	3	4	5	6	7	8	9	10	11	12	13	14	15	16	17	18	19	20	21	22	23	24	25
SAMPLE MEASUREMENT	1 90	97	118	108	112	105	106	102	106	100	102	121	108	107	106	96	102	103	105	103	94	92	107	89	112
MOVING RANGE, M R		7	21	10	4	7	1	4	4	6	2	19	13	1	1	10	6	1	2	2	9	2	15	18	23
NOTES																									

$\bar{X}$ = 103.6   UCL= 124.4   LCL= 82.9

INDIVIDUALS

UCL x   LCL x $\bar{X}$

145 — 130 — UCLx 115 — 100 — 85 LCLx 70 — 55

$\overline{MR}$ = 7.8   UCL= 25.5   LCL= 0

MOVING RANGES

30 UCLMR 20 10 MR 0

9 INTERPRET THE CONTROL CHART.

The X-MR chart is interpreted using the basic control chart interpretation rules. Control chart interpretation is explained in depth in another section of these materials. However, a list of the basic rules for interpreting out-of-control conditions is shown below.

1. Any point lying outside the control limits.

2. Run of seven points:

    a. seven or more points in a row above or below the centerline
    b. seven or more points in a row going in one direction, up or down

3. Any nonrandom pattern, including the following typical cases:

   a. too close to the average
   b. too far from the average
   c. cycles

The example chart does not show any points outside the control limits on either the individual or moving range chart. However, on the moving range chart, seven points in a row (subgroups 5-11) are below the centerline, indicating that the system is out of control or unstable. In other words, special causes of system variation are present. These points should be further investigated by the team to determine the causes of the unexpected variation. In the example, the team identified the unusually low variation within subgroups 5-11 to be caused by testing a new ventilator weaning protocol in one of the 2 CICU pods. (When the special cause is identified, it should be written directly on the chart paper.)

When systems are declared to be stable, the control limits calculated previously are simply drawn onto new chart paper as subgroups continue to be collected. This will allow the process owner to make decisions about the system's stability as each new subgroup is plotted. New control limits are calculated only when a change is made to the system.

REMEMBER

1. An X-MR chart is for variables data in subgroups of one.

2. The system variability, or range, is found by comparing subsequent subgroups.

 GETTING THE MOST FROM X-MR CHARTS

Getting the most from X-MR control charts means **taking care in interpretation**. Since each dot on this type of chart represents an individual piece of data, if the data distribution is not normal, the chart may show runs or trends when none exist. It may be useful to make a histogram of the data once you have collected enough points to get an accurate picture of the distribution. If the distribution is non-normal, consider changing the sampling plan to generate data you can analyze with a subgroup of more than one and use an X̄-R chart. Even an X̄-R chart with a subgroup size of two is more powerful than an X-MR chart. Sampling cost may be contained by converting to a subgroup size of two while cutting sampling frequency in half.

223

Collect as many points as possible before calculating control limits. The fewer data points you have to construct an X-MR chart, the less sure you can be that the chart represents the variability of the whole system. The more data points you have before calculating control limits, the more reliable the analysis. Because most control chart paper has space for only 25 subgroups it has become common to calculate control limits after the 25th subgroup.

Because it does not use subgroups of more than one, the individual chart is not as sensitive to shifts in the data as the measures of central location used in other variables control charts. Realize, therefore, that this chart may not allow you the quick process feedback you expect from other control charts.

Insensitivity of the individual chart to shifts also means you should **pay particular attention to the moving range chart.** Points outside control limits on this chart may be your first indication of a shift. Even this advantage is tempered, however, by the fact that one high range reading is often followed by another. (This occurs because a single reading affects two moving range calculations—the difference between it and the point before it, and the difference between it and the point after it.)

Effective use of X-MR charts depends heavily on **good sampling techniques.** Variation in processes such as patient waiting time, satisfaction rates, cost per member per month and cost per case don't depend solely on the passing of time but also on how often and how much data the process being observed is producing. As a result, it is important to set sampling schedules according to time sequence rather than the calendar or clock. Variation in productivity will often produce a cyclic chart of high and low productivity when samples are taken over time.

We should also note that the X-MR chart is the only control chart whose control limits for individuals may be compared directly to engineering specification limits or customer requirements to evaluate system capability.

Despite shortcomings, X-MR charts are important because they provide a way to examine single sample results over time with the power of statistical thinking.

OTHER HEALTH CARE EXAMPLES:

- Cost per member per month, per case, per laboratory cost, per ER visit

- Time to admit

- Time to treat

- Time to return to work

- Waiting or transfer time

- Patient transport time

- Patient satisfaction ratings per individual patient or average per month

- Time between safety incidents

- Time between repeat C-sections

- Time between thoracic infections post CABG

- LOS for specific DRG

- Cost per case by provider

- Time it takes to transfer a patient

- Time in hours or minutes to clean a patient room (turnaround time)

- Time from diagnosis to treatment per patient

- Time in hours to obtain a STAT consult

- Time in days to obtain a consultation

- Monitoring surgery waiting times per patient

- Time in days to first diabetic appointment

- Pharmacy waiting time

- Time to complete medication distribution

- Lab turn around time: ETC urinalysis TAT (min)

- Patients seen per week or per month

- Surgical cases per month

- Consults per week

GLOSSARY

GLOSSARY

A_2 - A multiplier or weighting factor of $\overline{R}$ used to determine the control limits for the $\overline{X}$ portion of the $\overline{X}$-R chart.

A_3 - A multiplier or weighting factor of $\overline{s}$ used to determine the control limits for the $\overline{X}$ portion of an $\overline{X}$-s chart.

A_6 - A multiplier or weighting factor of $\overline{R}$ used to determine the control limits for the $\overline{X}$ portion of the $\overline{X}$-R chart.

Affinity diagram - A tool that helps a team generate and organize a large amount of information. The ideas are organized based on mutual characteristics.

Analytical statistical studies - Ones in which action will be taken on the process or cause-system that produced the data being studied, with the intent being to improve practice in the future. All data looked at is from past (historical) for the purposes of prediction and extrapolation into the future. The goal is to determine stability or non-stability, amount and type of variation for the purpose of taking action on the process that produced the data. Since there is no way to take a random sample of the future, random sampling and probability theory offer no help here. All samples are judgment samples. Does not use tests and intervals of statistical inference. The technique of preference is to analyze a sample of data taken over time for the purpose of extrapolation using the simple control chart. (*Advanced Topics in Statistical Control*, Wheeler, 1995)

Attributes data - Qualitative data collected on objects possessing a certain characteristic. For example, yes/no, good/bad, pass/fail, go/no go, number of nonconformities. This data is counted, not measured.

Attributes control charts - A family of control charts for plotting attributes data. (Includes p-, np-, c-, and u-charts.)

Average moving range - The central location of subgroup moving ranges on the range chart of an X-MR control chart. Its symbol is $\overline{MR}$.

Average standard deviation - The central location of subgroup standard deviations on the s-chart of the $\overline{X}$-s control chart. Its symbol is $\overline{s}$.

Average range - The central location of ranges. It is found by averaging the individual ranges from a set of subgroups. It is represented by the dark center line on the Range chart. Its symbol is $\overline{R}$.

Average subgroup size - An average of all the subgroups on the control chart. It is found by summing all the subgroup sizes and dividing by the number of subgroups taken (k). Its symbol is $\overline{n}$.

Average median - The central location of subgroup medians on a X-R chart. Its symbol is X̃.

B₃ - A multiplier or weighting factor of s̄ used to determine the lower control limit for the s-chart.

B₄ - A multiplier or weighting factor of s̄ used to determine the upper control limit for the s-chart.

Bar chart - A graph with bars (rectangles) of different heights to show and compare data.

Baseline data - Data collected at the beginning of an improvement project. It is compared with future data collected on the same system to measure improvement.

Benchmarking - A word with multiple meanings.
1. The practice of finding and adapting best practices to improve organizational performance using a Plan-Do-Study-Act cycle to test the impact of adapting the "best practice."
2. Comparing one organization's performance to another.
3. The continuous process of measuring products, services, and practices against the toughest competitors or those companies recognized as industry leaders.

Bias - Something that influences the selection of certain items for a sample.

Bimodal - Said of a distribution having two modes. On a histogram, this condition is reflected by two "peaks" or high points.

Brainstorming - A creative process performed by a group to generate ideas on a certain topic. The members of the group use their collective thinking power to gather information about a problem. Each idea is written down.

c - The symbol for the number of nonconformities such as defects per subgroup.

c-chart - An attributes control chart that is used to monitor the number of nonconformities such as defects per subgroup. The subgroup size remains constant as the data is gathered.

C & E diagram - See cause-and-effect diagram.

CABG - Coronary artery bypass graft.

Capability analysis - A set of statistical calculations performed on a set of data to assess how the data distribution compares to specifications or requirements.

Capability analysis sheet - A manual worksheet for calculating process capability. It can be used with variables data, either normally or non-normally distributed.

Capability - The capability of a process is how the process performs compared to its specification limits or requirements.

Cause-and-effect diagram - A tool for individual or group problem-solving that uses a graphic description of the various system elements to analyze potential sources of system variation or causes to a problem. Also known as a fishbone diagram or Ishikawa diagram.

Centerline - A dark horizontal line drawn on the control chart to represent the average or central location.

Central location - The location of the center of a set of data points. Mean, median, and mode are the statistics that describe it.

Chart - See control chart below.

CICU - Coronary intensive care unit.

Change - To make different. Change includes transition, substitution, re-direction, design, re-design, improvement, and innovation. All improvement requires change, not every change is an improvement.

Check sheet - A data gathering device for gathering and organizing information. The check sheet format is a function of the situation for which it will be used.

Common cause - A source of variation that is inherent in the system and is predictable. A common cause of variation affects all the individual values of the system output being studied. A common cause of variation can be eliminated only by altering the system.

Conceptual population - Including the past and future operation of a process when speaking of the process' population.

Control chart - A graphic tool created by Walter Shewhart. The chart begins with a plot of statistical data over time. It shows the data plots, a central line, and one or two control limits.

Control limits - Lines on a control chart used as a basis for judging whether variation from subgroup to subgroup is due to special or common causes. These limits are calculated from system data, not set by engineering or management.

Correlated - Two variables are said to be correlated if they have a relationship. In other words, one variable will change when a change occurs in the other variable.

Correlation coefficient - A number produced from regression analysis that describes the strength of the relationship between two variables. This number ranges between -1 and +1. Its symbol is r.

Cp - A capability index which tells how well a system can meet two-sided specification limits, assuming that the average is centered on the target value. Large Cp's indicate less variation, compared to the specifications.

Cpk - A capability index which tells how well a system can meet two-sided specification limits. The system does not have to be centered on the target value for this index to be useful. Large Cpk's indicate less variation as compared to the specifications.

Crawford slip method - A method for generating ideas, the Crawford slip method minimizes internal group influences. Ideas are written on cards in silence rather than said aloud as in traditional brainstorming.

Criteria - A set of tests or rules applied to an object and used as the basis for a decision.

Cumulative percent line - On the Pareto diagram, the final line drawn to represent the cumulative percentage of the categories.

Cumulative frequency - In a frequency table, the cumulative frequency of a category is its frequency added to the frequencies of all the other categories above it.

$\bar{c}$ - The symbol for the average on a c-chart.

Customer - Anyone for whom an organization provides goods or services. Customers can be internal (co-workers) or external to the organization.

d_2 - The weighting factor used to calculate the estimated population standard deviation for capability analysis.

D_3 - A multiplier or weighting factor of $\bar{R}$ used to determine the lower control limit for the range chart.

D_4 - A multiplier or weighting factor of $\bar{R}$ used to determine the upper control limit for the range chart.

Data gathering plan - A plan (usually in the form of a matrix) which describes the process of collecting specific data. The plan includes what data to collect, how it will be collected, how much to collect (subgroup size), how often to collect it (sample frequency), where to collect it, methods to use, and who will collect the data. The form also includes an area to record issues of stratification such as time, location, symptom, and type.

Decision matrix - In Nominal Group Technique, an alternate technique for final selection of actions to be taken. A decision matrix is a worksheet of rows and columns, listing potential actions in the left column and selection criteria across the top row.

Defect - An occurrence such as a blemish, scratch, burn, error, or omission that appears on an object. A defect does not necessarily make the object unusable or unacceptable.

Defect location check sheet - A check sheet used to collect attributes data when it is important to know where a defect occurs on the item as well as the defect type. This check sheet begins as a drawing or sketch of the item being evaluated, a flow chart of the process, or a sample of paperwork forms.

Defective - Said of a product or service flawed beyond use or acceptability. Operational definitions must describe a product or service as either defective or not, with no gray areas in between.

Dependent variable - In a scatter diagram, the variable that is expected to respond to changes in the independent variable. The dependent variable is plotted on the vertical axis of the scatter diagram.

Deployment flow chart - A picture of a process that includes who is responsible, or deployed, to carry out each task in the process.

Digit - A whole number from zero through nine.

Dimensions of quality - Different viewpoints for defining quality in order to better match a product or service to a customer need. The dimensions include, performance, features, time, reliability, durability, uniformity, consistency, serviceability, aesthetics, personal interface, flexibility, harmlessness, perceived quality, and usability.

Driving forces - Forces which currently exist and help to bring about change.

Drop shadow - A darkened shadow behind a symbol in the flow chart. It is used to "zoom" a step in the flow chart. It indicates that another flow chart exists for the "zoomed" step.

DRG - Diagnostic related groups. Groups used to classify or code medical care for reimbursement purposes.

E_2 - A multiplier of the average moving range ($M\overline{R}$) used to determine the control limits for the individual chart.

ER - Emergency room.

Enumerative studies - One in which action will be taken on the material in the frame studied. The aim is to find out how many (errors) or how much of some trait exists in the frame and then to take action on that set of data itself. The aim is not to find out why there are so many or why there is so much. Uses random sampling, probability theory and statistical inference. (*Advanced Topics in Statistical Control*, Wheeler, 1995)

Estimated standard deviation - The estimation of the population standard deviation for capability analysis. The estimated standard deviation is found by dividing $\bar{R}$ by d_2.

Fishbone - See cause-and-effect diagram.

Flow chart - A picture of a process (sequence of events, steps, activities, or tasks).

Force field analysis - A planning tool that helps generate actions to implement a change. The tool is based on the idea that driving forces and restraining forces must be considered in any proposed change.

Frame - A list of all the elements in the population under study.

Frequency - The number of times a specified event occurs.

Frequency distribution - The arrangement of data into classes or interval groups.

Frequency table - A columnar table to record the frequency of occurrence of different events in increasing order of occurrence. The table has a column to record the frequency for each event and a column for cumulative frequency.

Grand mean - The central location of subgroup averages. It is found by averaging individual subgroup means. The grand mean is represented by a dark center line on the control chart. Its symbol is $\bar{\bar{X}}$.

Histogram - A bar chart that represents the frequency distribution of data. The height of the bars corresponds to the number of items in the class and the width of the bar corresponds to a measurement interval.

HMO - Health maintenance organization.

ICU - Intensive care unit.

Implementation plan - The output of force field analysis. It is a set of actions designed to increase the chances that change will occur.

Independent variable - In a scatter diagram, the variable that is believed to influence the other. The independent variable is usually plotted on the horizontal axis.

Ishikawa diagram - See cause-and-effect diagram.

JCAHO - Joint Commission on Accreditation of Healthcare Organizations. An accrediting body for health care organizations and a major influence on the health care industry.

Judgment sample - A sampling plan based on the opinion of an expert.

k - The symbol for the number of subgroups on a control chart.

Layout flow chart - A picture of how people and/or materials move through the physical environment where the process occurs.

LCL - The symbol for the lower control limit on a control chart.

LOS - Length of stay.

LSL - The symbol for the lower specification limit for a process.

MDC - Major Diagnostic Codes.

Measure - To collect quantifiable data about a dimension of performance of a function or process. (Source: JCAHO, performance improvement definitions)

Measures - Outcomes of a measurement process.

Measurement - The systematic process of data collection, repeated over time or at a single point in time. (Source: JCAHO, performance improvement definitions)

Moving range - The difference between consecutive subgroup values on an X-MR chart. The moving range is used as the measure for variability. Its symbol is MR.

$\overline{MR}$ - The symbol for the average moving range.

n - The symbol for subgroup size. A subgroup of five items is denoted as n = 5.

Negative correlation - In a scatter diagram, the relationship between two variables is such that as one increases, the other decreases.

Negative cause-and-effect diagram - A cause-and-effect diagram made for the opposite effect of what is preferred. Negative cause and effect is useful to generate many causes to be avoided if the positive effect is to be reached.

Nominal group technique - A problem-solving tool used to help teams generate ideas and choose the best one. It includes brainstorming.

Non-normal distribution - Any data set that does not show a normal bell-shaped distribution.

Normal distribution - A theoretical distribution of data whose shape is bell-shaped and symmetrical. It is the underlying distribution for variables control charts.

np - The symbol for number of items possessing a characteristic of interest.

np-chart - An attributes control chart that plots the number of items possessing a characteristic of interest in a constant subgroup size.

n$\bar{p}$ - The symbol for the average or centerline on an np-chart.

$\bar{n}$ - The symbol for average subgroup size.

OR - Operating room.

Operational definition - A clear, concise, and detailed definition of a measure. It includes the characteristic of interest, measuring instrument, method of test, and decision criteria.

Outcome - The result of the performance (or nonperformance) of a function or process(es). (Source: JCAHO, performance improvement definitions)

Outlier - On a histogram or scatter diagram, a point that does not fall into the pattern of the others.

p - The symbol for proportion of items possessing a characteristic of interest.

p-chart - An attributes control chart for plotting the proportion of items possessing a characteristic of interest.

Pareto diagram - A bar chart for ranking aspects of a problem. Typically, a few aspects make up a significant portion of the problem, while there are many trivial aspects.

People coordinate - A series of connected boxes drawn horizontally across the top of the deployment flow chart. Each box contains the name of the person, department, or division involved in the process.

Population - The area under study; opposed to a sample (see sample).

Positive correlation - A relationship between two variables such that as one increases, so does the other.

Probability paper - Graph paper designed for drawing a distribution curve.

Process - An action, or series of actions, that transform inputs from a supplier into outputs for a customer.

Process flow chart - A picture of the flow of materials through the sequence of steps required to make, move, store, and inspect items.

P_{ZLSL} - The symbol for the estimated proportion of output located outside the LSL.

P_{ZUSL} - The symbol for the estimated proportion of output located outside the USL.

$\bar{p}$ - The symbol for average proportion of items possessing a characteristic of interest, or the average of the p-chart.

Process owner - The person who coordinates the various functions and work activities at all levels of a process, has the authority or ability to make changes in the process as required, and manages the processes end-to-end so as to ensure optimal overall performance.

Quality - The ongoing matching of need with product or service.

r - The symbol for the correlation coefficient. See the previous definition.

R - The symbol for range. See definition for range.

RN - Registered nurse.

Random sample - A sample that allows every item in a population to have an equal chance of being selected.

Range - An estimate of spread in a set of data points; the difference between the highest and lowest values in the data set.

Rational subgroup - Multiple items sampled in a small region of time, space, or product. The purpose of rational subgrouping is to minimize variation within the subgroup.

Regression analysis - A statistical technique which allows one to produce an equation to describe a line that most nearly fits the points plotted on a scatter diagram.

Relations diagram - A pictorial representation of a problem and the aspects which make up the problem. It allows one to analyze the relationships of the aspects and determine a root cause and effect.

Restraining forces - Organization forces which currently exist and resist change. These forces are identified in a force field analysis.

Root cause - The main cause of a problem. In the relations diagram, the root cause is the element that has the most number of arrows leading out.

Root effect - The element of a problem that is affected most by the root cause. In the relations diagram the root effect is the element with the greatest number of arrows leading in.

Run chart - Data plotted on a line graph over time; used to detect patterns in the data.

$\bar{R}$ - The symbol for the grand range on a range chart.

Sample - The actual data gathered for quantitative analysis of a system, as opposed to population (see population). A small part of the total universe under study, intended to represent the characteristics of the whole.

Sampling - A tool that guides the quantitative study of a system; literally, the process of selecting the size and frequency of samples to be taken.

Scaling factor - The width or value of each division of the total length of an axis on a graph. Also called the "increment value" in scaling.

Scaling - Numbering or labeling the lines of a control chart or other graph in order to plot the points.

Scatter diagram - A statistical tool that plots the values of two variables on a graph in order to study the extent of the relationship between the two variables.

Skewed - Said of the shape of a distribution that tails off to one side.

Special cause - A source of variation that is unpredictable and occurs sporadically. When special causes are present, a system is said to be out of statistical control or unstable.

Specification limits - Boundaries (set by management, engineering, or customers) within which a system must operate; a detailed description of requirements.

Stable system - A system free of special causes of variation; this system is also said to be in control. The variation within a stable system is due to common causes, and is predictable.

Stakeholder - Any individual, group, or organization that will have a significant impact on or will be significantly impacted by, the quality of the product or service you provide.

Standard deviation - A statistic that describes the variation or spread within a data set.

STAT - (Latin) Sta 'tim (at once).

$\hat{\sigma}$ - The symbol for the estimated standard deviation.

Statistics - Numerical data used to describe a process based on subgroup data. Mean, range, standard deviation, median, and mode are examples of statistical data.

Stratify - To arrange or divide data into various configurations in order to understand sources of variation.

Subgroup - One or more occurrences or measurements taken at one time; multiple subgroups are used to analyze the performance of a system. Also known as sample.

$\bar{s}$ - The symbol for the average standard deviation on the s-chart of an $\bar{X}$-s control chart.

Supplier - The source of information, materials, knowledge or services that serves as input to a process. Suppliers can be internal or external to an organization.

TAT - Turn around time.

Target value - The exact value on which management, customers, or engineering want the system to operate.

TB - Tuberculosis.

Top-down flow chart - A picture of a process which shows each major step in the process broken down into its three to five essential tasks in each step.

u - The symbol for the number of nonconformities per unit in a subgroup; plotted on a u-chart.

u-chart - An attributes control chart that monitors the number of nonconformities per unit; can be used for variable subgroup sizes.

UCL - The symbol for the upper control limit on a control chart.

Unstable system - A system that contains special and common causes of variation; this system is also said to be out of control. An unstable system is unpredictable and cannot be improved until the special causes of variation have been addressed.

USL - The symbol for the upper specification limit for a process.

UTI - Urinary tract infection.

URI - Upper respiratory infection.

$\bar{u}$ - The symbol for the average on a u-chart.

Value - The customer's perception of the worth of a product when considering both the quality of a product and it's price.

Variation - The difference in results obtained in measuring the same phenomenon more than once. The sources of variation are grouped into two major classes: common causes and special causes. (Source: JCAHO, performance improvement definitions)

Variables control chart - A family of control charts for plotting variables data. (Includes $\bar{X}$-R, $\tilde{X}$-R, $\bar{X}$-s, and X-MR.)

Variables data - Quantitative data in the form of a measurement—for example, length, height, temperature, density, weight, time.

$\overline{X}$ - Represents the mean or average of a set of data points. This symbol is used to indicate the subgroup average on an $\overline{X}$-R control chart or the centerline on an X-MR control chart.

$\tilde{X}$ - Symbol for the median, the middle point of a data set arranged from low to high.

$\overline{\overline{X}}$ - The symbol for the grand mean.

$\tilde{\overline{X}}$ - Symbol for average of the medians.

X-MR control chart - A variables control chart which uses the individual data reading from a subgroup of one to chart central location and the range between consecutive subgroups to chart the system variability.

$\overline{X}$-s control chart - A variables control chart that uses the subgroup average to chart central location and the subgroup standard deviation to chart system variability. The subgroup size for this chart is usually ten or larger.

$\tilde{X}$-R control chart - A variables control chart that uses the subgroup median to chart central location and the subgroup range to chart system variability. Subgroup size must be larger than one and is typically an odd number less than ten.

$\overline{X}$-R control chart - A variables control chart that uses the subgroup average to chart central location and the subgroup range to chart variability. The subgroup size for this chart must be larger than one and is typically less than ten.

Z - The symbol for the number of standard deviations to the right or left of the average corresponding to any value in a normal distribution; used in capability analysis.

Z_{LSL} - The symbol for the Z value for the lower specification limit side of the curve. It represents the number of standard deviations between the average and the lower specification limit.

Z_{min} - The minimum of the absolute value of Z_{USL} and Z_{LSL}. It is used to calculate the Cpk index in capability analysis.

Zoom - To draw a drop shadow behind a symbol in the flow chart. It indicates that a detailed flow chart is drawn for that step.

Z_{USL} - The symbol for the Z value for the upper specification limit side of the curve. It represents the number of standard deviations between the average and the lower specification limit.

REFERENCE LIST

REFERENCE LIST

American Society for Testing Materials. *ASTM Manual on Quality Control of Materials.* American Society for Testing Materials, 1951.

Batalden, P.B. and Stoltz, P.K. "A Framework for Continual Improvement of Health Care." *Joint Commission Journal Quality Improvement.* 19: 424-447, 1993.

Berwick, D.M., Godfrey, A.B., and Roessner, J. *Curing Health Care.* San Francisco, CA: Jossey Bass, 1990.

Berwick, D.M. "The Clinical Process and the Quality Process." *Quality Management Health Care.* 1(1): 1-8, 1992.

Brassard, Michael. *The Memory Jogger Plus.* Methuen, MA: GOAL/QPC, 1989.

Buffa, Elwood S. *Modern Production Management.* New York: John Wiley and Sons, Inc, 1969.

Burr, James T. *SPC: Tools for Operators.* Milwaukee: Quality Press, 1989.

Chambers, David S. and Wheeler, Donald J. *Understanding Statistical Process Control.* Knoxville, TN: Statistical Process Controls, Inc., 1986.

Cleary, Michael J., et al. *Transformation of American Industry.* Dayton, OH: PQ Systems/QIP, Inc., 1986.

_____. et al. *Total Quality Transformation.* Dayton, OH: PQ Systems Inc., 1991.

_____. et al. *Total Quality Tools.* Dayton, OH: PQ Systems Inc., 1995.

Continuing Process Control and Process Capability Improvement. Corporate Quality Education and Training Center, Detroit: Ford Motor Company, 1987.

Delbecq, Andre L., Van de Ven, Andrew H., and Gustafson, David H. *Group Techniques for Program Planning.* Middleton, WI: Green Briar Press, 1986.

Deming, W. Edwards. *Sample Design in Business Research.* New York: John Wiley & Sons, 1953.

_____. "Notes." Conference at the University of Colorado, August 7, 1987.

_____. "On the Distinction Between Enumerative and Analytic Studies." *American Statistical Association Journal*, June 1953, vol. 48, pp. 244-255.

_____. "On the Use of Judgement Samples." *Reports of Statistical Applications*, March 1976, vol. 23, pp. 25-31.

_____. *Some Theory of Sampling*. New York: Dover Publications, Inc., 1966.

_____. *Out of the Crisis*. Cambridge: Massachusetts Institute of Technology, 1986.

Duncan, Acheson J. *Quality Control and Industrial Statistics*. Homewood, IL: Irwin, 1974.

Freund, John E., Perles, Benjamin M. and Williams, Frank J. *Elementary Business Statistics: The Modern Approach*. Englewood Cliffs, NJ: Prentice-Hall, 1988.

Fuller, F. Timothy. "Eliminating Complexity from Work: Improving Productivity by Enhancing Quality." *National Productivity Review*. Autumn, 1985.

Gitlow, Howard, Gitlow, Shelly, Oppenheim, Alan, and Oppenheim, Rosa. *Tools and Methods for the Improvement of Quality*. Boston, MA: Irwin, 1989.

_____. *The Deming Guide to Quality and Competitive Position*. Englewood Cliffs, NJ: Prentice-Hall, 1987.

Gitlow, Howard and Process Management International, Inc. *Planning for Quality, Productivity, and Competitive Position*. Homewood, IL: Dow Jones-Irwin, 1990.

Grant, Eugene T. and Leavenworth, Richard S. *Statistical Quality Control*. Fifth edition, New York: McGraw-Hill, 1980.

International Business Machine Corporation. *Process Control, Capability and Improvement*. Southbury, CT: The IBM Quality Institute, 1984.

Ishikawa, Kaoru and Lu, David J. *What is Total Quality Control? The Japanese Way*. Englewood Cliffs, N.J.: Prentice-Hall, 1985.

_____. *Guide to Quality Control*. Tokyo, Japan: Asian Productivity Organization, 1982.

Joint Commission on Accredition for Healthcare. *Comprehensive Accreditation Manual for Hospitals: The Official Handbook.* Bethesda, MD: Joint Commission on Accredition for Healthcare, Healthcare Organizations, 1997.

King, Bob. *Hoshin Planning: The Developmental Approach.* Lawrence, MA: GOAL/QPC, 1989.

Kume, Hitoshi. *Statistical Methods for Quality Improvement.* Tokyo, Japan: Association for Overseas Technical Scholarship, 1985.

Mizuno, Shigeru. *Management for Quality Improvement: The Seven New QC Tools.* Cambridge, MA: Productivity Press, 1988.

Scherkenbach, William. *The Deming Route to Quality and Productivity.* Rockville, MD: Mercury, 1988.

Scholtes, Peter R. *The Team Handbook.* Madison, WI: Joiner Associates, Inc., 1989.

Small, Bonnie S. et al. *Statistical Quality Control Handbook.* Indianapolis, IN: AT&T Technologies, 1985.

Tickel, Craig M. "Interpreting Process Capability." Dayton, OH: PQ Systems, Inc.

Tribus, Myron. "Quality First: Selected Papers on Quality and Productivity Improvement." Alexandria, VA: National Society of Professional Engineers, 1987.

_____. *Deployment Flow Charting.* Los Angeles: Quality and Productivity, Inc., 1989.

Western Electric Handbook Commitee. *Statistical Quality Control Handbook.* Indianapolis, IN: AT&T Technologies, 1985 printing.

Wheeler, Donald J., *Advanced Topics in Statistical Process Control.* Knoxville, TN: SPC Press, 1995.

_____. *Understanding Variation.* Knoxville, TN: SPC Press, 1993.

Wheeler, Donald J. and Lyday, Richard W. "Evaluating the Measurement Process with Control Charts." *Understanding Statistical Process Control.* Series 2, No. 1, Knoxville, TN, 1984.

TOTAL QUALITY TRANSFORMATION
VISUAL TOOLS GLOSSARY

Affinity Diagram: the organized output from a team brainstorming session.

c-Chart: an attributes control chart for plotting the number of nonconformities per subgroup. The subgroups must all be the same size.

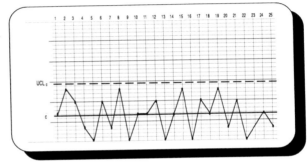

Capability Analysis: a set of statistical calculations performed on a set of data in order to determine the capability of the system.

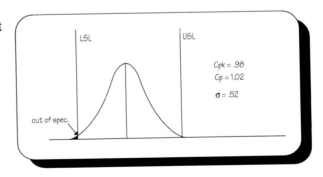

245

Cause & Effect Diagram: a picture of various system elements that may contribute to a problem.

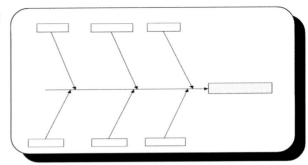

Check Sheet: a tool for collecting data in a logical format.

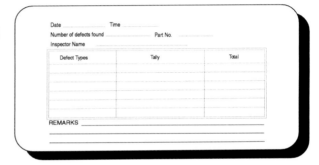

Control Chart Interpretation: the process of analyzing the control chart to understand the performance of the system being studied.

No Graphic

Flow Chart: a picture of any process (sequence of events, steps, activities, or tasks) which transforms inputs into outputs in a system.

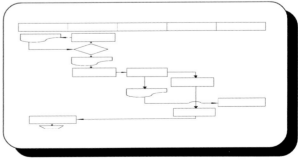

246

Force Field Analysis: a problem-solving tool used to analyze the driving and restraining forces that surround a proposed change.

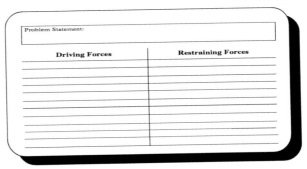

Histogram: a bar graph of raw system data. Shows basic information about the data, such as central location, width of spread, and shape.

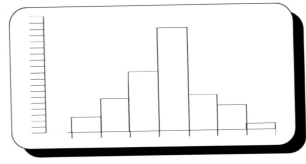

np-Chart: an attributes control chart for plotting the number of nonconforming items per subgroup. The subgroups must all be the same size.

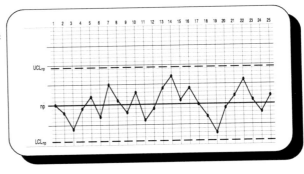

Nominal Group Technique: a structured group process used to help make decisions.

No Graphic

Operational Definition: a
clear, concise, and detailed
definition of a measure.

No Graphic

p-Chart: an attributes
control chart for plotting the
proportion of
nonconforming items per
subgroup. The subgroups
may be the same or of
different sizes.

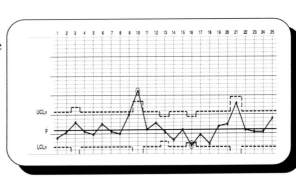

Pareto Diagram: a bar
chart which ranks related
measures in decreasing
order of occurrence.

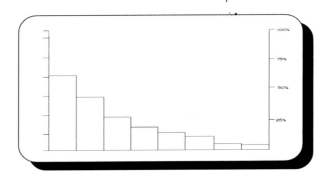

Relations Diagram: a
pictorial representation of
the cause-and-effect
relationships among the
elements of a problem or
issue.

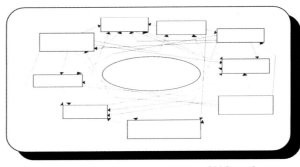

Run Chart: a line graph of data plotted over time.

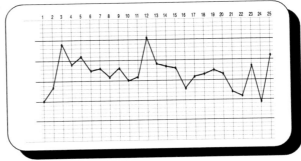

Sampling: a process which guides the quantitative study of a system.

No Graphic

Scatter Diagram: a graph showing the pairs of plotted values of two factors, one that is believed to be independent and the other dependent.

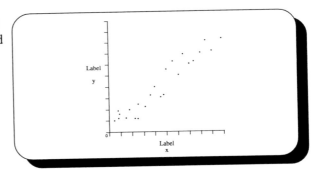

Systematic Diagram: a graphic representation of the different levels of actions used to accomplish a broad goal.

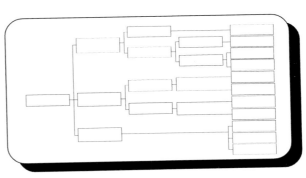

Reference List

u-Chart: an attributes control chart for plotting the number of nonconformities per unit in a subgroup. The subgroups may be the same or of different sizes.

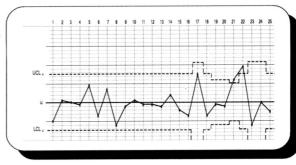

X̄-R Chart: a variables control chart for plotting the mean (or average) and range of subgroups. The subgroup size must be larger than one.

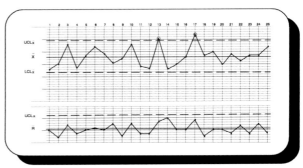

X̃-R Chart: a variables control chart for plotting the median and range of subgroups. All the values for each subgroup are plotted on the X̃-chart. The subgroup size must be larger than one.

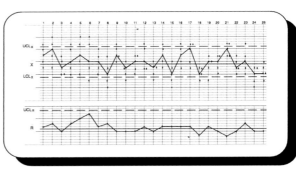

X̄-s Chart: a variables control chart for plotting the mean (or average) and standard deviation of subgroups. Generally used for a subgroup size of ten or larger.

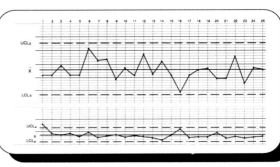

250

X-MR Chart: a variables control chart for plotting data in subgroups equal to one.

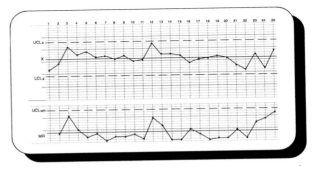

APPENDIX

Standard Normal Table

or

z	x.x0	x.x1	x.x2	x.x3	x.x4	x.x5	x.x6	x.x7	x.x8	x.x9
4.0	.00003									
3.9	.00005	.00005	.00004	.00004	.00004	.00004	.00004	.00004	.00003	.00003
3.8	.00007	.00007	.00007	.00006	.00006	.00006	.00006	.00005	.00005	.00005
3.7	.00011	.00010	.00010	.00010	.00009	.00009	.00008	.00008	.00008	.00008
3.6	.00016	.00015	.00015	.00014	.00014	.00013	.00013	.00012	.00012	.00011
3.5	.00023	.00022	.00022	.00021	.00020	.00019	.00019	.00018	.00017	.00017
3.4	.00034	.00032	.00031	.00030	.00029	.00028	.00027	.00026	.00025	.00024
3.3	.00048	.00047	.00045	.00043	.00042	.00040	.00039	.00038	.00036	.00035
3.2	.00069	.00066	.00064	.00062	.00060	.00058	.00056	.00054	.00052	.00050
3.1	.00097	.00094	.00090	.00087	.00084	.00082	.00079	.00076	.00074	.00071
3.0	.00135	.00131	.00126	.00122	.00118	.00114	.00111	.00107	.00104	.00100
2.9	.0019	.0018	.0018	.0017	.0016	.0016	.0015	.0015	.0014	.0014
2.8	.0026	.0025	.0024	.0023	.0023	.0022	.0021	.0021	.0020	.0019
2.7	.0035	.0034	.0033	.0032	.0031	.0030	.0029	.0028	.0027	.0026
2.6	.0047	.0045	.0044	.0043	.0041	.0040	.0039	.0038	.0037	.0036
2.5	.0062	.0060	.0059	.0057	.0055	.0054	.0052	.0051	.0049	.0048
2.4	.0082	.0080	.0078	.0075	.0073	.0071	.0069	.0068	.0066	.0064
2.3	.0107	.0104	.0102	.0099	.0096	.0094	.0091	.0089	.0087	.0084
2.2	.0139	.0136	.0132	.0129	.0125	.0122	.0119	.0116	.0113	.0110
2.1	.0179	.0174	.0170	.0166	.0162	.0158	.0154	.0150	.0146	.0143
2.0	.0228	.0222	.0217	.0212	.0207	.0202	.0197	.0192	.0188	.0183
1.9	.0287	.0281	.0274	.0268	.0262	.0256	.0250	.0244	.0239	.0233
1.8	.0359	.0351	.0344	.0336	.0329	.0322	.0314	.0307	.0301	.0294
1.7	.0446	.0436	.0427	.0418	.0409	.0401	.0392	.0384	.0375	.0367
1.6	.0548	.0537	.0526	.0516	.0505	.0495	.0485	.0475	.0465	.0455
1.5	.0668	.0655	.0643	.0630	.0618	.0606	.0594	.0582	.0571	.0559
1.4	.0808	.0793	.0778	.0764	.0749	.0735	.0721	.0708	.0694	.0681
1.3	.0968	.0951	.0934	.0918	.0901	.0885	.0869	.0853	.0838	.0823
1.2	.1151	.1131	.1112	.1093	.1075	.1056	.1038	.1020	.1003	.0985
1.1	.1357	.1335	.1314	.1292	.1271	.1251	.1230	.1210	.1190	.1170
1.0	.1587	.1562	.1539	.1515	.1492	.1469	.1446	.1423	.1401	.1379
0.9	.1841	.1814	.1788	.1762	.1736	.1711	.1685	.1660	.1635	.1611
0.8	.2119	.2090	.2061	.2033	.2005	.1977	.1949	.1922	.1894	.1867
0.7	.2420	.2389	.2358	.2327	.2297	.2266	.2236	.2206	.2177	.2148
0.6	.2743	.2709	.2676	.2643	.2611	.2578	.2546	.2514	.2483	.2451
0.5	.3085	.3050	.3015	.2981	.2946	.2912	.2877	.2843	.2810	.2776
0.4	.3446	.3409	.3372	.3336	.3300	.3264	.3228	.3192	.3156	.3121
0.3	.3281	.3783	.3745	.3707	.3669	.3632	.3594	.3557	.3520	.3483
0.2	.4207	.4168	.4129	.4090	.4052	.4013	.3974	.3936	.3897	.3859
0.1	.4602	.4562	.4522	.4483	.4443	.4404	.4364	.4325	.4286	.4247
0.0	.5000	.4960	.4920	.4880	.4840	.4801	.4761	.4721	.4681	.4641

TABLE OF WEIGHTING FACTORS

Subgroup Size	A_2	A_3	A_6	B_2	B_4	d_2	D_3	D_4	E_2
2	1.880	2.659	1.880	0.000	3.267	1.128	0.000	3.267	2.660
3	1.023	1.954	1.187	0.000	2.568	1.693	0.000	2.574	1.772
4	0.729	1.628	0.796	0.000	2.266	2.059	0.000	2.282	1.457
5	0.577	1.427	0.691	0.000	2.089	2.326	0.000	2.114	1.290
6	0.483	1.287	0.548	0.030	1.970	2.534	0.000	2.004	1.184
7	0.419	1.182	0.509	0.118	1.882	2.704	0.076	1.924	1.109
8	0.373	1.099	0.433	0.185	1.815	2.847	0.136	1.864	1.054
9	0.337	1.032	0.412	0.239	1.761	2.970	0.184	1.816	1.010
10	0.308	0.975	0.362	0.284	1.716	3.078	0.223	1.777	0.975
11	0.285	0.927	0.350	0.321	1.679	3.173	0.256	1.744	
12	0.266	0.886		0.354	1.646	3.258	0.283	1.717	
13	0.249	0.850		0.382	1.618	3.336	0.307	1.693	
14	0.235	0.817		0.406	1.594	3.407	0.328	1.672	
15	0.223	0.789		0.428	1.572	3.472	0.347	1.653	
16	0.212	0.763		0.448	1.552	3.532	0.363	1.637	
17	0.203	0.739		0.466	1.534	3.588	0.378	1.622	
18	0.194	0.718		0.482	1.518	3.640	0.391	1.608	
19	0.187	0.698		0.497	1.503	3.689	0.403	1.597	
20	0.180	0.680		0.510	1.490	3.735	0.415	1.585	
21	0.173	0.663		0.523	1.477	3.778	0.425	1.575	
22	0.167	0.647		0.534	1.466	3.819	0.434	1.566	
23	0.162	0.633		0.545	1.455	3.858	0.443	1.557	
24	0.157	0.619		0.555	1.445	3.895	0.451	1.548	
25	0.153	0.606		0.565	1.435	3.931	0.459	1.541	
More than 25		$3/\sqrt{n}$		$1 - 3/\sqrt{2n}$	$1 + 3/\sqrt{2n}$				

ATTRIBUTES CHARTS

np	$UCL_{np} = n\bar{p} + 3\sqrt{n\bar{p}\left(1 - \frac{n\bar{p}}{n}\right)}$ $LCL_{np} = n\bar{p} - 3\sqrt{n\bar{p}\left(1 - \frac{n\bar{p}}{n}\right)}$	c	$UCL_c = \bar{c} + 3\sqrt{\bar{c}}$ $LCL_c = \bar{c} - 3\sqrt{\bar{c}}$
p	$UCL_p = \bar{p} + 3\sqrt{\frac{\bar{p}(1-\bar{p})}{n}}$ $LCL_p = \bar{p} - 3\sqrt{\frac{\bar{p}(1-\bar{p})}{n}}$	u	$UCL_u = \bar{u} + 3\sqrt{\frac{\bar{u}}{n}}$ $LCL_u = \bar{u} - 3\sqrt{\frac{\bar{u}}{n}}$

VARIABLES CHARTS

$\bar{X}$-R	$UCL_{\bar{X}} = \bar{\bar{X}} + (A_2 \times \bar{R})$ $LCL_{\bar{X}} = \bar{\bar{X}} - (A_2 \times \bar{R})$ $UCL_R = D_4 \times \bar{R}$ $LCL_R = D_3 \times \bar{R}$	X-MR	$UCL_X = \bar{X} + (E_2 \times M\bar{R})$ $LCL_X = \bar{X} - (E_2 \times M\bar{R})$ $UCL_{MR} = D_4 \times M\bar{R}$ $LCL_{MR} = D_3 \times M\bar{R}$

SYSTEM IMPROVEMENT

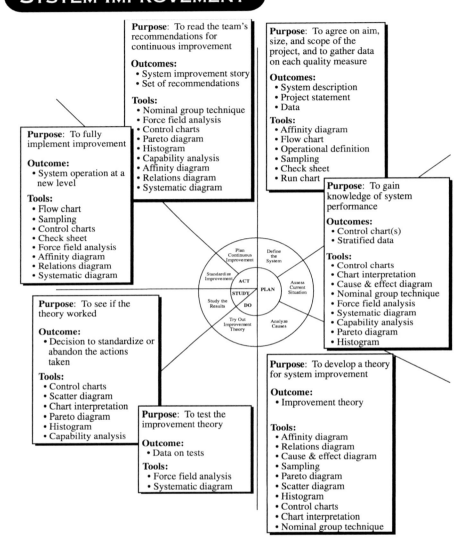

Purpose: To read the team's recommendations for continuous improvement

Outcomes:
• System improvement story
• Set of recommendations

Tools:
• Nominal group technique
• Force field analysis
• Control charts
• Pareto diagram
• Histogram
• Capability analysis
• Affinity diagram
• Relations diagram
• Systematic diagram

Purpose: To agree on aim, size, and scope of the project, and to gather data on each quality measure

Outcomes:
• System description
• Project statement
• Data

Tools:
• Affinity diagram
• Flow chart
• Operational definition
• Sampling
• Check sheet
• Run chart

Purpose: To fully implement improvement

Outcome:
• System operation at a new level

Tools:
• Flow chart
• Sampling
• Control charts
• Check sheet
• Force field analysis
• Affinity diagram
• Relations diagram
• Systematic diagram

Purpose: To gain knowledge of system performance

Outcomes:
• Control chart(s)
• Stratified data

Tools:
• Control charts
• Chart interpretation
• Cause & effect diagram
• Nominal group technique
• Force field analysis
• Systematic diagram
• Capability analysis
• Pareto diagram
• Histogram

Purpose: To see if the theory worked

Outcome:
• Decision to standardize or abandon the actions taken

Tools:
• Control charts
• Scatter diagram
• Chart interpretation
• Pareto diagram
• Histogram
• Capability analysis

Purpose: To test the improvement theory

Outcome:
• Data on tests

Tools:
• Force field analysis
• Systematic diagram

Purpose: To develop a theory for system improvement

Outcome:
• Improvement theory

Tools:
• Affinity diagram
• Relations diagram
• Cause & effect diagram
• Sampling
• Pareto diagram
• Scatter diagram
• Histogram
• Control charts
• Chart interpretation
• Nominal group technique

(Center cycle diagram labels: Plan Continuous Improvement, Define the System, Standardize Improvement, ACT, Assess Current Situation, PLAN, STUDY, DO, Study the Results, Try Out Improvement Theory, Analyze Causes)

SYSTEM IMPROVEMENT

This seven-step process is based on the Plan-Do-Study-Act Cycle (PDSA). It should be used when a system exists and needs significant improvement or the current system is not meeting customer needs. This process is typically used by cross-functional teams that need to solve a problem and require a method to measure their success. This process is most useful if the system being studied has already been standardized and stabilized.

SYSTEM ALIGNMENT

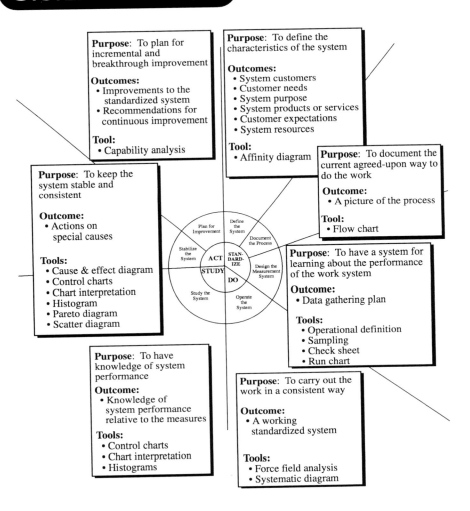

SYSTEM ALIGNMENT

This seven-step process is used for aligning or standardizing work systems. The alignment process is used when a system is confusing, inconsistent, complex, error-prone, or hard to learn. System alignment is the method by which everyone in an organization can apply quality principles and practices to the work he or she does every day. It is typically used by functional work teams. System alignment is sometimes called daily management, process management, or quality in daily work.

Appendix

Set of Calculations for Capability Analysis

$$\hat{\sigma} = \frac{\bar{R}}{d_2}$$

$$Z_{USL} = \frac{USL - \bar{\bar{X}}}{\hat{\sigma}}$$

$$Z_{LSL} = \frac{\bar{\bar{X}} - LSL}{\hat{\sigma}}$$

Capability Indices

$$C_{pk} = \frac{Z_{min}}{3}$$

$$C_p = \frac{USL - LSL}{6\hat{\sigma}}$$

Complete Formula to Find the Standard Deviation of Subgroups

$$s = \sqrt{\frac{\Sigma (X - \bar{X})^2}{n - 1}}$$

INDEX

INDEX

R

r
glossary 236
R 192, 196
glossary 236
range 196, 197, 199, 201
bar 197
correlation coefficient 188
glossary 231
random
distribution 115
sample
glossary 236
range (R)
calculation of 196
glossary 236
rational subgroup
glossary 236
regression analysis 188
glossary 236
relations diagram
glossary 236
restraining forces
glossary 236
root cause 54
glossary 236
run chart 153-161
glossary 236

S

sample 164
glossary 237
sampling 163-174, 224
glossary 237
scaling 37, 141, 157, 180, 199. *See* chart
glossary 237
factor
glossary 237
scatter diagram 59, 175-190
glossary 237
skewed
distribution 115, 116
special cause 64, 107, 133, 205

glossary 237
specification limits 194, 224
glossary 237
spread 124
stability 10, 65, 151, 154, 192, 210. *See* assess stability
stable system 71
glossary 237
standard
deviation 119, 125
glossary 237
standardization 11, 41, 90
statistics 73, 96, 118, 195
glossary 237
stratify
glossary 237
data 10, 40, 205, 210
subdivisions 146
making 108-109
subgroup 146, 156, 169, 172, 192
glossary 237

T

target value
glossary 238
top-down flow chart
glossary 238
tree diagram. *See* systematic diagram
Tribus, Myron 91, 96

U

u 34
glossary 238
number of nonconformities per unit 4
chart 4, 15, 34, 42-49, 75
glossary 238
UCL 6, 37
glossary 238
c 36
MR 214, 217, 221
np 6, 8
p 17, 19
R 197
u 48
X 215, 221

undercontrol   2, 32, 64
uniform distribution   115
unstable system
 glossary   238
USL
 glossary   238

V

variables
 control chart
  N>1 ($\overline{X}$-R)   191-208, 255
  N=1 (X-MR)   209-225, 255
  glossary   238
 data   10, 42-43, 82, 108, 128,
 156, 172, 205, 212
  glossary   238

W

weighting factors   217, 255
Western Electric   216
Wheeler, Donald   6, 197, 216

X

X-double bar
 grand mean   254
X-MR   67, 125, 194, 210
 glossary   239

Z

Z value
 glossary   239
 LSL
  glossary   239
 min
  minimum of the absolute value of
   Z_{USL} and Z_{LSL}
  glossary   239
 USL
  glossary   239
zoom   99
 glossary   239